TINSEL
WILDERNESS

By John Klawitter

DoubleSpin Press

DoubleSpin

Cover Art by Deron Douglas

www.derondouglas.com

Edited by Marilyn Peake

ISBN: 0983037299
ISBN-13: 9780983037293

DEDICATION

To my wife
Lynn Jensen-Klawitter
who was there
from the Burnett times,
who saw it all
and added
the magic ingredients—
love and laughter

CONTENTS

FOREWARD

Tinsel Wilderness is one of the most inspirational books I've read in a very long time. As I read one after another of his lessons on how he survived as a creative person, I felt like an explorer having come upon treasures, or a kid on Christmas morning.

John Klawitter remarked in an email to me, "Everyone has at least one story...the story of their life." In this book, he meets the challenge head-on of extracting the important threads from individual events in his life and weaving them into stories about himself and the famous and not-so-famous people he has known in show business and the advertising industry. Within each story, the reader will find wisdom and life lessons as rich as solid gold.

--Marilyn Peake, Author & Editor
www.marilynpeake.com

"Frogs ain't funny!"
--Bill Hanna

"Because I say so and *I'm me* and *you're you*!"
--Card Walker CEO of Disney

"The secret is Chinese grandmothers."
--Arthur Pierson, Director

"I like the one with the picture of me."
--Dustin Hoffman

"How come you never pitch us
any more of your ideas?"
--Joe Barbera

"Get out of my sight!"
--Carl Hixon, Burnett

"Sorry, *his* people are coming in …but go
away and we'll give you a couple shows."
--Bob King, Disney

"What the hell do you think *you're* doing?!"
--Richard Harris, Kelly-Nason

"Get off my set!"
--Jack Clayton

"And don't you come back no more!"
--Peter Douglas

First Flight

I remember the day Cornelia Otis Skinner came to town to "declaim upon the stage" as her mimeographed one-sheet billboard declared. There she was up on that theatrical poster in all her grandeur, one arm thrown dramatically in the air as she gazed off into some distant horizon only she might see. This was back in the time of hot rods and bobby socks, and the grand old lady of the theater was due to sweep down past the dark and sooty brickworks, the tall, black-belching chimneys and rusting junkyards into our town of Chicago Heights like a pale spirit from a long-forgotten era, the time of Victorian gentility, to cast a few civilized lines to the intellectually impoverished sons and daughters of the working class. The grimy puddle of our reality offered the Hotpoint factory, the Ford body stamping plant, the DeSoto Paint Company, Victor Chemical, Acme Tool & Die Works, Industrial Welding, and the Inland Steel mill where they melted down old railroad tracks and turned them into new re-bar and steel fence posts. We didn't have much in the way of dramatic recitals.

I was the eldest son of a loving, alcoholic welder and a strict, rosary-thumbing mother who saw God's hand in all events; I was gawky, dreamy and nearsighted, a somewhat less-than-average teenager who loved to lose sight of himself in books of romance and high adventure. In Darkest Africa. The Coming of Cassidy. A Princess of Mars. Daredevils of the Air. The Virginian. I had this ant-horde of brothers and sisters, and due to the economic necessities of existence at that level, was destined for a short scholastic career followed by a hot and lusty career in the steel mills, or perhaps at my father's side in the welding firm. In my dreams I may have been holding the wheel to drive the pirate schooner, sails fully set and cutting through the waves across a churning ocean, but in the real world I was rowing my dinghy across a muddy pond, preordained to paddle out my days filling paint cans with *Aztec Tan* latex or *Peppermint Green* oil base, bolting fenders on Falcon body frames or catching new iron up on the fiery hotbeds where the furnaces roast your skin and the cherry red re-bar is spun.

This special one-night event was a one-woman show, entirely Cornelia, and would feature poetic readings--and short excerpts from dramatic pieces, to boot! Very intense for the time and place, which was 1956 in the Bloom Township High School auditorium. I don't know that I'd have thought to go, but that was my sophomore year and I was in Speech class, and Mrs. Wilson stood at her desk with her spectacles down around the end of her nose and declaimed it a mandatory attendance.

Today I remember this tall, stately lady standing in a pool of light emoting in her tremulous voice, "Ghost Lake's a dark lake...a deep lake...and old..." She also did Lady Macbeth's bloody hands scene, "Out, out, damned spot!", and to tell the truth that's about all I

10

remember. It didn't matter; the pieces themselves weren't what I found important about Cornelia Otis Skinner. It was the fabric, not the text. I was hearing the great roar and the little whispers of actual life up there in front of those lights. I didn't have the words or the understanding for it back then; all I knew was that I was experiencing something big, real big, *mighty* big.

After the show, Mrs. Wilson led the Speech and the Drama classes backstage as a special privilege. I was surprised to see that Cornelia may have been grand, but she certainly wasn't that old--maybe in her mid-fifties. There I was, bare wrists hanging out of last year's shirt, wide-eyed under a cowlick of unruly hair that no Vaseline Tonic could ever tame, chalky scuffed white suede shoes under my frayed roll-cuff jeans. I stood right next to her, still as a statue, hardly daring to breathe as she *took a few questions* from her admiring fans. *Is what you do hard?* a freshman girl in pigtails asked. *Where do you go next?* The others crowded around. *Did you ever act in a movie?* I just stood there, frozen under the hot orange stage lights in the electricity of the moment like a humble fly in amber while Cornelia politely answered as best she could. She smelled slightly of sweat and greasepaint, and there was something wonderful about her, I'm not sure what...to this day, I'm not sure what...I do know that there was a moment when, in her reflected light, to me all things seemed possible and even the iron manacles of absolute reality could be questioned as if they might, like the chains of gravity holding John Carter, Prince of Mars, magically fall away.

And then Mrs. Wilson tugged at us like so many little boaters, reminding us the magic hour was over. I was bewildered. Time had never slipped by so fast. I could see the auditorium was nearly empty. *Amazing!* For a moment I didn't budge. Old Mrs. Wilson smiled sympathetically, and I saw she was looking directly at me. "It's not a life for any of you," she said firmly, and she shook her tired old mop of gray curls. *Not to be. It was not to be.* She was right; it was late, it was time to grab our noses and jump in the warm puddle and swim back to our safe little coves.

I tried to dog-paddle along with the rest, I'm sure I did. After all, the route was wide, clear and well traveled, and we were all taking it together. It was, after all, the only pond in sight and the only way to be taken. And yet somehow, in spite of all that help and good direction, I wasn't going to be able to make it back. I remember a turning--a sudden, irrational fury--and how I stared hard-eyed at poor, unknowing Mrs. Wilson, staring purposefully, like the Virginian had when he set aside his poker hand and said, "When you say that--*smile*", glaring until it was she who turned away. And looking back over all the years and all that has passed in between, I can recognize now that it was at this improbable moment that the impossible boat with its awkward rigging and all its outlandish airs, like a newborn bat or insect half-crazed with the first upward taste of flight, unfolded its gauzy wing-like sails and launched itself into the bright and shiny seas.

The Happy Jack Platter Shop

It's not a totally stupid idea to be a little nice to people. Of course, you wouldn't want to go overboard and become a kiss-ass, but there may be some benefit to occasionally improving your attitude toward the ordinary Joes and Janes around you. For one thing, by putting out harmonious vibrations, you maintain your karmic balance, which in turn enables your creativity to flow in a pure and steady stream unaffected by the negativity which is pulling the less-enlightened all around you down into the *merde*. Then too, you never know when the mailboy is going to be promoted to senior vice president in charge of creative--so you'd better be nice to him.

Once, in that very long-ago time when I was playing spy in Saigon, I met a Scotsman at the Bristol Bar, a fairly high-class South East Asian watering trough which, if my memory serves me correctly, was on the Street-of-Flowers near Le Loi. This Scot was blessed with a mop of that carrot-reddish hair only Scots have, and he spoke with such a burr that I could hardly understand him. Yet the poor, mad fool insisted he was a radio announcer. He had to say it three times before I even understood him. He was a *rrrrrrrrr-adio jock, mon*. What's more, he was leaving in three days for the highlands (Scottish, not Vietnamese), and if I wanted his job, it was mine.

Well, Ba Muoi Ba is one of the more powerful beers you can find in the Orient, and as the evening wore itself into a pleasant blur, my new life as a radio jock seemed a better and better idea. I remember that somewhere toward curfew my new friend Kevin confided that my American accent was every bit as ugly on the king's ears as his own was to me. Some confidence-builder, huh?

I staggered out of bed the next morning, grabbed my shoes and a cab and slept all the way down Pasteur Street to the radio station. Wonder of wonders, Kevin *was* there, just like he said he'd be. He showed me the ropes in about ten minutes, walking me around and introducing me as their new radio personality. Then he dragged me into the booth and we were on the air.

Now those deep-voiced fellows on the old Columbia School of Broadcasting commercials may have convinced you it takes a great deal of specialized training to get up in front of that microphone, but that's all a lot of hogwash. Hey. Not necessary at all. Look, the pilot dies in the air, you learn to fly the plane. And the next morning I showed up alone. Wahoo. Look, ma, no hands!

This was a couple of years before Adrian Cronauer had his Good Morning, Vietnam show, and I wasn't on Air Force Radio, either. We're talking about good old VTVN, a real native radio station. Our signature was a scratchy 78 rpm of the *William Tell Overture* somebody had swiped from the Canadian Broadcasting System. The girls who spun my platters wore slit-skirted silk ao-gai, chewed betel nut and ducked under the table whenever they heard the low rumble from the B-52's shellacking the provinces, convinced it was the ghosts of their dead ancestors.

I called my show The Happy Jack Platter Shop. We had a simple format; I'd do 15 minutes of news, and then spin 15 minutes of records that I'd mostly scammed from the guys back in the barracks. The music was easy, but the news was a little more complicated.

The stories came clacking off the teletypes from AP and Reuters, just like it does in newsrooms around the world. As it was in English, a Vietnamese government interpreter translated it back to the native tongue for their political department (read "censors" here). Offending passages were cut out with a scissors, and what was left over was given back to the station interpreter, Mr. Van Nguyen, who translated it back into his own chop-socky brand of English. Sometimes it seemed like an afterthought. It was mind-numbing stuff, often without even a tenuous relationship to the original stories. I had about 20 minutes to smooth the most obvious craters and manholes, and to give it a few run-throughs, and then I was on the air.

Little Van Nguyen was a pest from the get-go, with his heavy dandruff, sour-whiskey breath, a little potbelly hanging out over the beltline of his cheap suits, and the cigarettes dangling from one corner of his mouth in the negligent French manner. I guess I'd known him about a week when he first started bugging me for a Pentax from the PX. He carried on about this practically nonstop from the moment we got to the station. He would gladly pay me 100 P to the dollar instead of the official rate of 80. (I could get 200 from any cigarette lady on any street corner, and 230 at Johnny's Bookstore.) He would be happy even with the smaller Pentax, the less expensive one without the wonderful zoom lens that could be such a help in his business and might in fact make his career. He would never, ever bother me for anything ever again from the PX, except possibly for some hairspray, lipstick and maybe a bottle of perfume for his wife's birthday or some chocolate candies for his kids for Christmas.

I was managing to keep my temper with Van Nguyen, but just barely, when the weak Phan Huy Quat government was overthrown. That morning I was just lucky enough to catch the Grey Snail off-base before the U.S military declared an orange and shut down the gates. My bus passed ARVN tanks in the streets and machine gun nests at corners some military genius had decided were strategic. The cabbies were still running-- hell, they ran right through the Tet offensive--and so I was able to flag a ride from MAC-V over to the station.

When I got there the newsroom was deserted, but there was a stack of neatly clipped translations on my desk. If possible, they were more nonsensical than ever:

President Johnson reassured [blank space] yesterday. The American people can be confident [big blank space]. In the interim, the valiant fighting effort of the courageous Vietnamese people goes on.

Top Strategists met in Hawaii to [huge blank space]. The valiant peoples of Vietnam should be reassured by this.

[Blank space] farm crops [blank space] product of the cooler weather. [Enormous blank space] resulting in lower prices and an excellent result.

[Blank space] new American wave of comedians [big blank space].

Nothing at all about the collapse of the government.

Still, Van Nguyen had clearly been and gone. At least I wouldn't have to listen to his miserable whining about the camera he wasn't going to get. I poured a bitter cup of coffee from the pot, scooped up the tattered copy and headed for the booth. Before I knew it, *William Tell* was jangling in my ear, and then I picked my way through the news, mostly making it up as I went along:

Top strategists and allies of the Vietnamese peoples, including the U.S., Australia, New Zealand and South Korea, met in Hawaii to review the war effort and find new ways to apply pressure to the hated enemy, the Viet Cong and their masters in North Vietnam. The generals read a personal message from President Johnson and then issued a statement for reporters gathered from around the world that the war was going well, and it was only a matter of time before the ultimate Viet Cong surrender.

I turned the second news item--the cut up farm story--into an informative discussion of the pineapple industry, and went on to do a little color piece on the Smothers Brothers, those happy, bumbling American folk-singer comedians.

Hey, no problem, this show was nearly in the bag. I had my feet up and was halfway through the music side--I remember Peter, Paul and Mary were singing "Lemon Tree, very pretty, and the lemon flower is sweet/ But the fruit of the poor lemon is impossible to eat" when a squad of khaki uniformed ARVNs burst through the door into the outside room where the turntables and the jittery *co-gai* were and started waving their machine guns around in the air.

I was then in my mid-twenties, but these soldiers were little more than kids. One of them figured out the magic of the soundproof double doors and made his way into the booth where I was. He jabbed his machine gun in my direction and said in almost inaccessible English, "You say Ong Quat a filthy pig?"

"Ahhhhh...nooooo...," I replied.

This didn't seem to make him happy. It probably was the wrong answer. "You say Ong Quat a filthy pig?" he repeated, turning the machine gun in a somewhat more operational way toward my face.

"Ahhh, maybe I did say *something*...", I stammered.

His face started to get red and he slammed off the safety on his weapon. I could see this kid hadn't been to Buddhist Patience School.

And then by some miracle the wonderful little Van Nguyen was there, holding up his hands and stepping in

17

between us. He yelled at the kid with the gun for a while in the sing-song way that Vietnamese have, and then turned to me. "It all a small mistake," he grinned with a little shrug. "This young fellow with gun here, he *want* you to say Ong Quat is a filthy pig." Van Nguyen gestured encouragingly to the mike, which was clicked off because Peter, Paul and Mary were still singing. "He not know we on air or not."

"Ohhhhh...", I said. I sat in my chair and cleared my throat.

My rousing condemnation of the old government seemed to satisfy everyone. After the show I did a few chits and chats with the kids in khaki. One of them insisted on taking a group shot of us all with his battered little Kodak, and I even signed an autograph on the back of a napkin. I waved goodby and walked swiftly down the big marble staircase. I was out the front door and hailing a cab before I knew it, just happy to still be sucking air.

That afternoon--and I would have done it sooner but the PX didn't open until noon--I ran over and bought my dear friend Van Nguyen his Pentax. Not the cheap model, the expensive one with the big black zoom hanging on the front that just might make his career.

Bennie Gallogrape

Back as far as the Neanderthal days at Bloom Township High School, I was writing and producing P.A. announcements for the Spring Fling, Homecoming and the SnoBall Dance and designing posters for the Clean-Up campaign. I guess it was only natural that, one day, I should try to get into advertising. After I earned a few college degrees and enlisted for three years in the army, I came back to Chicago and started looking around for a job with some sort of an advertising position lurking in the back of my mind. But I didn't have any contacts or role models in advertising, which meant I didn't have the foggiest notion how to go about it.

No matter who you are and who you know, it's *hard* landing that first job as a professional creative person. Even back then, there were forty or fifty applicants for every opening, so they hardly ever advertised in the papers. I didn't know about the occasional want ads in Advertising Age, but I had heard that Ad Agencies NEVER EVER hired their creatives from employment agencies. Employment agencies were considered the scum of the earth, and their workers were con men, shills and lackeys. (It is only in retrospect I realize this is because ad biz people, outcast by the news biz, the art world, and *real* show biz, relish the few groups that they can kick around.)

Young and ignorant, I circled the ads in the Chicago Tribune and started pounding the pavement, looking for anything in some way related to *the ad biz*. I told my mother I might not mind being in the rat race, because I was one of the rats. I turned down a position selling tube and sheet steel because my father had been in that business in a minor key way, and I didn't want anything to do with it. I turned down a job selling life insurance, because everybody had the founder's book on *positive living* on his desk. They told me how great it was, and they smiled and smiled, and it didn't seem natural. After ten minutes or so, nobody quit and it made me nervous wondering which face was going to break first. It wasn't going to be mine. I turned down a writing job with a paint factory when they told me I'd have to spend 30% of my time on the line, filling paint cans. Not that I minded filling paint cans...Lord knows I'd done my time at the DeSoto Paint Factory in Chicago Heights, one of those summer jobs to get through college; but I could see 30% really meant 80%.

I had the same problem everybody does who wants to get in the business--no experience. So I did what they always tell you--I created a batch of ads for clients real and imagined to show how good I was at thinking up advertising ideas. I shot a photo of a seagull sitting on a garbage can outside *Sal's Fish & Chips*, and wrote the headline, "Sal's Fish Are Fresher". Hey, I figured, *a gull knows.* Six or seven things like that.

I managed to show my samples to a half-dozen of the advertising giants of Chicago--Will Grant of Will Grant Advertising, and some folks over at Tatham, Laird & Kudner--and they all said the same thing, "Boy, you don't have any *experience*. You gotta go somewhere and write *catalog* advertising. That's the sure way to get your start, on the bottom. First you do *catalog*, then you do *small space newspaper for local clients*, then you do *local radio*, then after *some magazine and newspaper ads*, you work your way up to *national clients with radio and TV spots*. But you don't do nothing until you do *catalog.*"

So I went to Sears and Montgomery Wards and places like that, and they all told me that their stuff was too important, they *couldn't just hire a guy off the street to do catalog.*

At about this time, one way or another, I heard that the Chicago mega-agency Leo Burnett Advertising occasionally had openings for junior copywriters. I called, and, sure enough, they had a program where every blue moon they hired a would-be writer to run their film files department. After a year or two of cutting together 16 mm sample reels, building presentation tapes on quarter inch tape, running 35 mm film on interlock projectors and sweeping up the floors in film files, the trainee was expected to have learned enough about Burnett products and made enough contacts to where he could be hired by one of the Creative Directors.

I called and found out the trainee program was run by one of the head creatives, Pete Franz, who also was a very big deal on the Gallo account, and yes, Pete himself would interview me a week from Thursday. This sounded great, so I boned up on Burnett's client list and decided to do a storyboard for Gallo Wines, which had recently been written up in the business section of the paper as a very difficult and yet large and profitable account.

Now, although Leo Burnett the man, the myth and the legend, has said some wise things about advertising, and his company has shaped a lot of images over the decades, the men who toil there are sometimes looked down on for creating "Midwestern breadbasket" advertising with folksy characters: Farfel the Dog. The Jolly Green Giant. The Marlboro Man. Charlie Tuna.

The Pillsbury Doughboy. Kellogg's Tony The Tiger.
Snap, Crackle, Pop, Rice Krispies. The Keebler Cookie
Elves.

Those unruly Gallo Brothers, on the other hand,
were apparently using Burnett to hire fine artists and so
create some sort of snob appeal for their wines. I
decided that was laughable. What Gallo really needed
was more of the Burnett style image. And so I created
"Bennie Gallogrape" for them. Bennie was a plump,
energetic little guy who went around extolling the virtues
of the Gallo wines. I was going to write a jingle to go
along with my idea, but when I couldn't find anything to
rhyme with "grape" but "rape", I gave it up in favor of
some snappy dialogue between Bennie and these other
grapes who weren't quite so good but who also wanted
to be in Gallo wines. The spot ended with a gentle but
wise narrator telling us voice-over how all the grapes
want to be Gallo, but it's tough, things being what they
are in the premium wine business.

The grand meeting where I presented my
storyboard was attended by three or four middle-level
Burnett creatives, in addition to Pete Franz. One of
them rudely pointed out that Bennie Gallogrape owed
everything to Tom Rogers, the Burnett senior writer who
had created Charlie Tuna. As Tom was in the room, my
face was red as a beet. Pete came to my rescue, saying
that it was a "good, inventive knockoff", and if I'd used
the same dialogue in a Charlie Tuna spot, they'd all have
liked it. Tom said nothing, just smiled a little bit. Later, I
found out the three younger guys, all hotshot Assistant
Creative Directors, had voted against me, overruling
Tom and Pete.

So much for Burnett. I was walking down Michigan
Avenue, killing time until the electric came to take me
back south to where I was living in the old homestead,
when a guy waved at me from behind a desk in the
World Employment Agency. He was middle-aged and
bald, and his suit looked rumpled and shiny at his

elbows and the seat of his pants. I gave him a little wave and hurried on past. He came to the door and yelled, "Hey, you looking for a job?"

"Yeah," I said in a low voice, "but they don't want me."

The guy looked like a used car salesman. He hooked me by the lapel and tugged me into the office. It didn't take much. I was drifting in my sorrows like a piece of olive-green seaweed.

"Sit," he said. He pointed to a fold-up chair across from his desk. "Now. Who don't want you?"

"Leo Burnett don't want me."

He itched a scratch somewhere on his back. His shirt collar and sleeves were frayed, and there were dandruff flakes caught in the big catsup spot on his tie.

"How do you know?" he asked. He burped and I smelled garlic.

"I just was there. They said no."

"Who said no? You gotta name?"

"Pete Franz."

"*YOU* just talked to Pete Franz? What's *YOUR* name?"

I told him, adding that it didn't make any difference, Pete had already said no.

"No doesn't really mean no," the employment agency guy said. "Not all the time." He scratched under one arm, "Now, if I get you this job, they ain't gonna pay me. Do *YOU* agree to give me ten percent of your first year's wages?"

"Yeah, sure."

I signed the contract while he looked in a sloppy notebook and then dialed a number.

"Pete," my man said, scratching under his other arm with the rubber eraser end of his pencil, "you didn't give the guy a chance. You didn't even see half his stuff. I got it all out in front of me here. He's brilliant, I tell you--*brilliant!*"

Ten minutes later, I had another appointment at Burnett, this time to see Pete Franz without the three harpy Assistant Creative Directors. Two weeks after that I started as copy trainee in film files at the best agency in town. Six months after that, I was promoted to junior copywriter, working on Kellogg's cereals and Nestle Chocolates. In a few months I was writing radio and TV spots, working on new product development, and learning how to stick motion picture film together.

So don't let anybody tell you it can't be done, or give you rules on just how to do it. None of it means a thing. You can slam-dunk with your elbows, catch the pigskin with your feet and slide into first base backwards. You figure it out for yourself, whatever works. And keep on trying. Eventually, through a marvelous process known only to the few, the brave and the true--and now, you--even well-meaning but laughable grape dudes like Bennie Gallogrape and his grape buddies become transmogrified into the finest of wines.

Leo and the Three Ho's

Back before Don Imus got in trouble for emulating black street talk, the now-forbidden word "Ho" had an entirely different meaning. Sure, there was "Land Ho!", but I'm not even talking about that. I'm talking about Leo Burnett, the great copywriter, creative director and founder of the huge agency that today bears his name. When I heard about the trouble into which Imus dunked himself, for no logical reason my mind flashed back to the story of Leo and the Three Ho's.

Leo was entirely something else from the ordinary, run-of-the-mill creative, and even today the agency that bears his name won't let you forget it. It's hard to be a creative person, and even harder to grow from that position to being a good director of other creative people. You've got to teach your young writers and ACDs to write on target, on time and with wit and clean communication--time after time after time--and they've got to do all this without losing their imagination or enthusiasm for the job. Leo was a master of the difficult psychology of dealing with creatives. I don't know how he got that way; maybe he was born with it.

Leo's long gone and yet he was so good that even today he remains the agency's most precious asset--and they know it. Practically before new Burnett employees have a chance to settle on their bottoms in the training room, somebody from human resources will get up and start the Leo stories. What he said about Kellogg's Corn Flakes. How, when going down from blood sugar deficiency in a big meeting, he asked for a candy bar-- calling after the frantic gofer to make sure it was a Nestle's Bar...Nestle being a Burnett client. I was there as a young cub copywriter when old Leo gently chided us--*I don't care if you smoke or not, but if you do, make sure it's a Marlboro.* Generally, the tales are already legends within the organization and perhaps even the ad biz, a part of the *collective corporate culture.* And because the stories are told in a bright and witty way with a real snapper of an ending, both teller and listeners enjoy the telling. Problem is, it's all too easy to lose what I'll call *the basic meaning* of the tale, to forget just exactly why the old fart did what he did in the first place. It happens all the time.

Recently after a long, dusty day at the ranch, branding stray verbs and rescuing dangling participles, I was over at the Sagebrush Cantina lifting a few to moisten my parched throat when an account guy friend of mine came over to my table with a big problem. He'd been working directly with an art director to design a brochure. The art director, a young Picasso with lots of juice behind his wrist, naturally equated "the right corporate look" with a fate somewhere between being drawn-and-quartered and expiring from The Black Death. So he kept coming back with wildly creative solutions that were "out of the box", as they are inclined to say in the ad biz.

However, since the account guy vastly outranked this art director, he had finally been able to strong-arm him into a solution appropriate to the look and feel of the company. Only now it was boring, and they both knew it.

What to do, what to do? Should the account guy recapitulate, throw in his corporate socks, as it were--go back to the art department and admit defeat? That's the kind of problem that cagy old Leo Burnett, founder of the mega-agency that bears his name today, excelled at solving. Leo's three greatest contributions to the world of advertising were the clarity of his prose, his inherent drama theory (Great advertising will flow from your mind if you concentrate on the inherent drama of the product, that is, on that characteristic or benefit which makes it uniquely saleable), and the understanding way he handled creative people who worked with him.

One story they tell of Leo's ability to handle his creatives has to do with a long-standing Burnett client, that funny little pea company in Wisconsin. It happened this way: A team working on a campaign for the client's new line of frozen vegetables took their storyboards and quarter-inch sound tapes into a CRC (Creative Review Committee meeting) to present to Leo. This campaign was big stuff in the early 60's, when vegetables mostly came fresh or in cans. Anyone with vision could see that, if the agency did their job well enough, a whole new section would be added to grocery stores.

Leo listened quietly to the presentation, and at the end heaped praise on their efforts. At this time Leo was a short, rotund man, a balding little fellow with big bushy white eyebrows, and he always seemed so vulnerable, so *ordinary-man-on-the-street*. Still, the creatives knew how to read him, and they saw that his praise, while genuine, was one step from being over the top. Team Leader Bob Noel thought it over and finally asked, "What is it, Leo? What's bothering you?"

"Nothing," Leo said. "What do you think it is?"

"I don't know. Maybe we've been working with this too long and have gotten too close to it, but we all feel like we're just about there."

"I think you're almost there, too," Leo agreed. "That jingle is *great*...maybe, if anything, you just want to get a little more *Giant-ness* into it..." Leo didn't have any more to say, and the meeting broke up.

Bob Noel and his creatives got out of there and went back to that song like Spaniards after Incan gold. *Almost there, almost there, Leo had said it was almost there...* They played it over and over until one of them finally jumped up and said, "I've got it!" In the jingle, right after the famous refrain, *In the valley of the jolly Green Giant*, there were three French Horn notes on a descending scale. They took the instrumental notes out and replaced them with a hearty giant's voice singing HO, HO HO!, and, once again, advertising history was made. Frozen food took off like a rocket and grocery stores had to become supermarkets to hold, among other things, all the new frozen food products. Leo always gave Noel and his creative gang the credit for the song, and they in turn always gave him credit for the direction. Win-win, you know?

So, when the account guy came to me with his problem, I told him to go back to the art director and praise the latest efforts as being in the right direction, but to encourage him to find some way to take it over the top, to make it "even more" exciting and interesting. He was tremendously relieved and left the watering hole raving about how I was some sort of genius. I didn't tell him about Leo and the three Ho's. It's generally a good idea to let them think you've come up with these things yourself.

The Man Who Invented the Hamm's Beer Bear

It was about 15 years ago. I was thinking about Cleo Hovel the other day, so I called around town to see if I could pick up a little background on him. Cleo had been a big deal at Leo Burnett when I was there, and we once had a run-in that just may have changed my life, so of course every now and then I think about him.

A couple of old Disney hands didn't remember him at all. Bill Hanna, who I always think of as knowing everybody and everything about animation, only remembered the bear.

"Oh yeah," Bill said, "A bear that looked a little bit like Yogi, wasn't it?"

Wally Burr worked as a commercial producer at Burnett in the 60's when Cleo was there. At the time when I was asking around, Wally ran his own sound studio in North Hollywood where he recorded a lot of the voices that end up on Saturday Morning television and the syndicated cartoons. But all he remembered about

Cleo was, "He would draw caricatures of everybody on the napkins when we all went out to lunch."

I guess the lesson is, no matter what you do, make it count. Because in the end we all die alone, and aside from the three or four people who really knew us, the rest can only remember us by the things we leave behind...like our family and our work.

I remember Cleo Hovel. He was a middle-aged man with a roundish face and owl eyes behind big glasses. I think he was working on the Pillsbury Doughboy at the time, but he was introduced to me as "the man who created the Hamm's Beer Bear". Well, that was the chunky, clunky, chummy animated bear who sold billions of beers over the years, and all it takes is one hit like that and you're an advertising superstar for life. Witness Bill Bernbach and Volkswagen, Burt Manning and "When You're Out of Schlitz, You're Out Of Beer", Leo Burnett and the Hupmobile...well, maybe not Leo and the Hup, but it was Leo and a lot of things, for sure...Anyway, once you create something like that, the agency likes to show you off, clients want to chum around with you, and you've got a whole new lifestyle to contend with. Easy, for instance, to drift away from the animation table where you did your best creating.

I was hired by the Leo Burnett Company in 1965, fresh back from Vietnam; I hadn't yet "detoxified", as they say in the military rehab business, and so a lot of the world made even less sense than it does today. I was thrown in the tub with a bunch of other young writers. They were, generally speaking, aggressive, career oriented and dedicated to giving their bosses what they wanted. Slavishly on the mark, I called it. I, on the other hand, was vague, stubborn, impulsive and rebellious. I thought my job was to create things, and so I was into finger-painting logos, experimental filmmaking, cardboard cutout worlds, stop-motion animation, crazy spoof lyrics and a dozen other offbeat things. You know it had to be really out there, to be on the rim of the "far out" sixties; and if it was, there you'd find me, too. I guess I drove my boss, Carl Hixon, nuts in those days. I do know I had the reputation as the one guy who "absolutely wouldn't take directions".

Still, they used my stop-frame idea for the long-running Pop-Tarts campaign. And, with a little reworking, my daydream campaign for Nestle's Quik was a big score for another guy. My Nestle's Chocolate Village campaign became a reality and ran to the tune of $6 million, big numbers in those days. And they used an entire breakfast cereal commercial I shot on 16 mm-- only they went to Hollywood and re-shot it practically frame for frame. My slo-mo notions became the standard way to pour milk in the so-called "beauty shots" at the heart of every Kellogg's commercial, and my jingle "When the sun comes up in the morning, time for Raisin Bran" found its way into the Raisin Bran spots.

In spite of all those creative sparks, those weren't happy days for me. I was a junior copywriter competing with Carl-of-the-big-black-Porsche, Carl the Broadway song-and-dance dude who strolled through the halls of Burnett singing Gilbert & Sullivan lyrics, Carl who had brought Nestle's $100,000 candy bar back from the brink of extinction with a "Pal Joey" knockoff where the hoods all sing, "So do yourself a favor, Get the million-dollar flavor, In a $100,000 candy barrrrrrr!", Carl who handed out assignments to write commercials that he'd already written, sold the client and was heading for the West Coast to produce. Carl the Creative Director, my boss. There's only one way that confrontation's going to turn out.

Carl once asked me to film a scene for a coffee break at a big Kellogg's meeting. He said I could do whatever I wanted, and then he went on to describe what *he* wanted--a cafe scene where the waiter breaks a bottle of wine over a surly customer's head and the narrator says "Coffee Break". I thought that was a stupid idea, so without checking back with Carl, I animated a

31

cow by stop-framing the camera and making the cow's jaw go up and down. The cow turns his head to us and laconically says, "Coffee Break".

I thought it was funny, but when Carl saw it, I thought he'd have a cow of his own. He insisted we shoot his cafe scene, which, like I warned, did end up like a warmed-over shaggy dog joke. At least the Kellogg's people never saw it...because I got it out of the Chicago lab an hour too late. Carl blamed me, and the entire experience didn't do anything for male bonding, much less my long-range plans at the Leo Burnett Company.

Anyway, it was in these grim days when, coming back an hour late from lunch, I got in the elevator with Cleo Hovel. I was glaring mad, the way I still get when faced with the ridiculous, the stupid or the unfair, and Cleo must have thought I was disgusted with him.

"I know I've been drinking too much," he confessed. "But don't think I'm enjoying myself. Now my day is ruined. I'll get back to that damn board and I won't feel like working. I have to wine and dine and talk to all these clients. I have to do it. It's become my job. I've become my job. And now my job is becoming me."

It embarrassed me, him blathering on like that, but I wasn't much on explaining my feelings in those days. The elevator hummed, we were alone, and I stared at him, saying nothing.

And then, unexpectedly, he reached out and grabbed my wrist.

"Promise me you'll try your best not to let this happen to you," he said.

I was startled. I was more than alienated back then; I didn't like people touching me. Not anybody. I tried to pull away, but his hand was like a claw. I had to control myself to resist popping him one in the face with my free hand.

"Yeah. Okay," I said. "I'll try."

"Your best!" he insisted, still holding on and slurring the words so *best* sounded like *besht*.

"My best," I repeated.

He seemed to forget about me then, or maybe he was overwhelmed with his memories of creating the great bear. He retreated to the other side of the elevator and stared at the wall. We came to his floor, and the doors hummed open, filling me with blessed relief.

"See you," I said. He got out and walked away without another word.

That was the last time I spoke with the man who invented the Hamm's Beer Bear. He went up to Minneapolis and took over a big agency there. I didn't hear of any amazing new creatures who sold a billion of anything, so I suppose he was lost in his daily ritual of pleasing the clients.

I heard, about ten years later, that he was found dead in a motel room. Somebody from the front desk came up because his television set was blaring static in the middle of the night and they found him sitting in a chair, staring lifelessly at the fuzzy station I.D. on the TV screen.

These days, when I think about all that, I'm a little softer on my old enemy Carl. His ways seemed unfair and egotistical to me at the time, but at least he'd found a way to sing his song and still be in the game. If he was cruel, I was equally hardheaded, and I ended up learning a lot from him.

As for Cleo, he didn't change my life so much that I never had a drop of liquor after that. In fact, coming out of the lost generation, all of us so much affected by hard-living folk like Hemingway, Kerouac and Brautigan, I drank my share and paid the price for it. But I always tried to get in the day's work first, to do my ads, my ideas, my little pile of pages. Come on, who knows

why? I, myself don't...and yet, still today, there are times
when the old dog turns surly--when I refuse a lunch or
fail to meet a client after hours for drinks. Maybe I just
don't want to. On the other hand, maybe it's because I
feel the faint but insistent memory of Cleo Hovel's
clawed hand on my wrist, pulling me away. And my
mind forms words I never could have said in that
elevator years ago, *Here, Cleo--this one's for you.*

Tenacity in Art

If you're going to be any sort of a creative person at all, you've got to go at your particular discipline with cunning and perseverance. You've got to display *staying power*. Novelist James Michener talks about marshalling his forces like a general, and Picasso still was doing push-ups and chasing women in his 90's. A sense of humor doesn't hurt either, to get you through your days, which will, from time to time, be long and grim. Like my friend, artist-reporter Franklin McMahon, always says, "You've got to keep going, because if it's at all worthwhile, only one in ten people you show it to will ever really get what you're doing." Franklin should know; he's been translating his prolific drawing and painting talents to film for years, with varying degrees of success with critics and the public.

I first met him in 1967. I was in the bowels of the Leo Burnett Agency, busily mixing some quarter-inch sound tracks for a Kellogg's Corn Flakes presentation like it was the most important thing in the world, when he walked in with a few tapes he needed cut together. Franklin was wearing an English wool hat pulled low over his eyes, one of those heavy Irish sweaters and a wool scarf around his neck. He was maybe 45 or 50 years old, and he had a Midwestern twang to his voice. His eyes kept darting around the room, picking up details. I finished my Kellogg's spot and then had a go at "fixing" his tapes, a series of muddy *presences* he'd recorded from a trip he'd taken to Italy to paint his colorful impressions of the Vatican.

By that time, he'd already completed his first film, a 30-minute documentary, The Artist as Reporter, which showed how he'd grown from a court reporter to a guy who went out into life and drew scenes. He never drew anything from his imagination, and he was proud of it. If he'd drawn a scene, it existed somewhere. He was now far away from the courthouse, recording scenes that were pure reality, things like "Duck Hunting in Cairo", or "Scenes from the NFL", which he wanted to translate to the filmic medium.

I helped him with his sound tapes and they ended up in his second documentary, The World of Vatican II. One thing led to another and I ended up co-writing, co-producing and directing a 90-minute documentary with him, Scene Politic. We worked like dogs for over a year to pull Scene Politic together. Franklin followed the presidential candidates around, pausing to sit on a portable stool. There he'd be, sketching like mad while he let his tape recorder run between his legs. Those were the sad and chaotic times when Bobby Kennedy was assassinated, and the Democrats held their convention in Chicago with Mayor Daley holding sway on the convention floor while riots swirled through the South Side of the city. It ended badly, as you may remember, with Hubert H. Humphrey snatching the party nomination away from the people's choice, George McGovern, with some dubious maneuvering. The Republicans were in Miami, and Ronald Reagan, already looking old and leathery, would get beaten out by Richard M. Nixon while George Romney's assertion that he'd been brainwashed on Vietnam washed him out of the race and George Wallace made noises down south like he could move into the White House at any time with no problem at all. Interesting times, as the old Chinese curse says, and we made a film out of it.

Problem was, Franklin was recording history with a #2 medium soft pencil instead of a 16 mm Bolex, which was a little bit like shooting kamikazes off the deck of the Lexington with a blunderbuss. Not that there wasn't art, craft and taste to his work, but it was the age of *cinema verite*, the time of the hand-held and the zoom, when every kid with a camera was a *filmmaker*. Franklin's idea was to cross-pollinate the disciplines of realistic drawing and film. His notion brings up an entire range of interesting questions. *Would Frederic Remington have made a good animation director? If 24 frames per second is "full animation" and 12 frames per second is "Limited Animation" (a la television cartoon shows), can camera-moves-on-stills be considered any form of animation at all? Is a painting simply one frame, a snapshot as it were, of the moving picture of life? Were paintings ever meant to be filmed in the first place?*

As his director, I quickly realized there were certain problems which pained him perhaps more than anybody; he worked very quickly, yet a "major drawing" might take him six or eight hours to sketch and color in. Cutting and panning around on that drawing, we might only be able to get ten or twelve seconds of film out of it. He would eye me sadly, and say something wistful, like, "Gosh, there's *a lot of paint* in that sketch..."

Worse yet, American audiences have always been used to *action*. There was something calming and insightful about panning around on a bunch of Franklin's drawings, but people looked at our footage and kept thinking it was just the opening gambit, the color, the preview of the live action footage which was to come. After a few minutes, they would get twitchy. Hey, this is a problem, we've got 90 minutes here...

When we had our first hour in the can, Franklin proposed that we should go to New York, to pitch the programming folks at the networks. He'd made friends with a guy who worked for CBS named Sam Zelman, and Sam was ready to line us up with the big boys. I remember that meeting very well; CBS was trying to figure out what they were going to do for their upcoming election coverage, and the interest in the room was intense. The lights dimmed and all eyes were riveted to the screen...at least, for the first three minutes. Then they started to talk to each other, right over Franklin's narration and the sound background we'd labored on for months. They argued about their next meeting, joked about somebody's new pair of shoes, decided where they were going to have lunch. Easy to see we'd lost them.

Even today, network programmers have the imagination of a fly and the attention span of an Irish Setter, and I should have known better than to dare to hope for a network sale--but I was fresh to the game and I'd pinned high hopes on the presentation, and as we walked out of the screening room I felt crushed and bitter.

Franklin, taking one look at my face, tried to console me. He clapped me on the back and said, "I tell you, Jack--it just proves my theory. No matter how good you are, when you're trying something new and different, there's only one guy in ten who ever really gets it. One guy in ten. We've just got to keep looking until we find that guy." He paused and a pixie-like grin came over his face, "Of course, our problem is there's *only three networks*..." We got on the elevator laughing, the laughter of the doomed.

In a way, McMahon was right. ABC, NBC and CBS all passed on the project, calling it too slow-moving to our faces and artsy-fartsy behind our backs. On the other hand, our work did run nationally. It took NET, the national educational television network, to finally "get" it. They picked up on Scene Politic, and the entire 90 minutes ran from coast to coast a couple of nights before the election. The numbers were very large for a non-major network show, and we got letters thanking us for "performing a service to the nation", summing up in a nonpartisan way what all the candidates had said on the long campaign trail. To top it off, Franklin and I won an EMMY and a trunkful of other awards.

In spite of that exposure and success, as a medium of expression, Franklin's idea of mixing realistic drawings and film never really caught on with the mass market. It didn't seem to matter; he figured he was on to something, and so he kept at it, no matter what. I did one more film with him, the 26-minute World Cities, which combined drawings he did around the world recording how people globally were moving from the rural to the urban. I left for Hollywood and he went on to repeat Scene Politic four years later, but '72 was a dull election, and so the film was only shown locally. Franklin continued to build up his body of art/film work; he did a long documentary on the trial of The Chicago Seven Vietnam War dissenters, and a half-hour Christmas in Chicago which has become a minor classic in that town, running every Holiday Season on WGN.

None of those later films ever ran nationally, nor did they make Franklin a lot of money. But, in an odd way, they are not at all dated. They seem as fresh today as they were when they were first created. They give the viewer an insight into the way things were at the particular time and place, perhaps an even sharper look than can be gotten from looking at stacks and stacks of old newsreels. My guess is, Franklin's film work will be around at least as long as Albrecht Durer's plates or Honore Daumier's sketches. And isn't that what real art is all about?

The Navajos Water the Desert

After they finished their spaghetti western, the Italians moseyed out of Indian Country leaving a half-mile of railroad tracks stretched from nowhere to nowhere across the Painted Desert like a misguided Railroad Brothers of America attempt at surrealism or another silly, pompous *Cristo was here*. So I guess the Navajos were ready for us when my producer, Danny, and I and a couple of cameramen descended on them from Hollywood to do our low-budget 15-minute educational film about how the Navajos bring water to the desert.

I assured my Navajo friend, Jimmy Shorty, that we didn't have any tracks, Italians or spaghetti in our little epic; and I brought along a few forbidden cases of beer to grease the skids of local government. We got permission and drove his big water-drilling rig down the twisting, unpaved road into Monument Valley. This was flinty John Wayne and steel-chinned Randolph Scott country, the tortured red sandstone lands much beloved by those who present real history to moviegoers in the form of shoot-'em-ups and ride-'em-downs. We finished our descent and moved deeper into the sand-and-brush valley, conscious that we were a part of this history. At least I did. Danny was too busy yelling at the Indian driver to hurry up, and Jim Shorty was outside the cab, throwing big boulders under the back wheels to keep the rig from sliding over the edge of the steep and narrow road.

I guess the one thing I hadn't explained to the Indians was about Danny. He was born poor, one of about eleven kids in a broken family. He married at 16 and had three kids of his own in three years. You'd think a guy like that would lose himself in booze and self-pity, but Danny saw his one chance at fame and fortune, and leapt for it like Tarzan after the last vine. Film production knows no limits for those with brass balls and a little luck, and for a while Danny had plenty of both. By this time he'd proven everybody wrong, and was clawing his way up through middle management at a mid-sized Hollywood studio. All that remained was to see how high he could go.

There was a lot to admire in Danny, but he hadn't gotten to where he was by standing still, and being around him was like leaning into a whirlwind. He would work 18-hour days, sleep at his desk and push himself and his staff on through the weekends. He was the stuff of which ulcers are made. His mouth was a running canker sore, and he was a constant reminder that there was always somebody ready to work harder, faster and for less. All of which meant that, at the fresh young age of 21, he didn't listen to anybody, and he pushed at everybody.

If General Custer had been looking for an aide-de-camp, Danny would have been the man. All of which ran 180 degrees contrary to the kick-back Navajo way of life we had stumbled into. The Navajos would still be enjoying the morning sunrise while, if it wasn't spectacularly filmable, Danny had gone on to breakfast, or was setting up a shot somewhere else.

In the first few days, we'd had several minor altercations with the Indians. Danny couldn't understand how the huge drilling rig could only get two miles to the gallon and he had to make a big deal out of it, accusing the Indians of stealing; I had to explain in reality it consumed *two gallons to the mile.* He didn't have much patience for waiting while the rig idled 15 minutes of "his" gas away so a herd of sheep could cross the road. The Indians who ran the rig didn't want to work the long hours Danny demanded until I got them time and a half for overtime, and that was a big hassle until Danny saw the light: It was time and a half or no rig at all. Then Danny nearly got himself and a helicopter pilot killed, baiting the pilot until he flew too near the side of a mesa and was sucked into a downdraft. I was pleased to see my young producer came back a little chalk-faced from that one; perhaps the guy wasn't *beyond learning* after all.

Jimmy Shorty and the Indians reported to me, because they felt they couldn't talk to Danny. Danny resented it, because on paper he was my boss. Hell, he'd bought my script and hired me to direct. And here the savages were, listening to me instead of him. It was just another layer of pressure for me; somehow day after day staggered by, with us filming in the desert heat of day and the blowing sands that came up at dusk.

We finally were ready for the all-important scenes where we were to strike water. Jimmy explained to us that when they struck water at shallow depths, the water never gushed up like an oil well. In fact, it had to be pumped up. I had the old familiar sinking feeling until he told us he had a method where they could "backwash" water from a big tanker-truck through the system and it would shoot high in the air just like a gusher. We set out to capture this phenomenon with as many cameras as we could. My cameraman and I were doing the master shot, the second cameraman was going to do a fancy slo-mo down-shot from high in the rig as the water gushed up to fill his frame.

Danny'd started in the film business pretty much as I had, by doing everything himself. He resolved to set up a third camera and personally run it. Enthused by the fancy slo-mo shot, he thought he could do it one better. Jimmy had explained the mechanics of what was to happen; in addition to the vertical gusher, there was one big 8-inch pipe on the side of the truck from which a stream of water would come out like a cannon shot. It was at this point that Danny wanted to set up his camera.

I thought that might be okay, and suggested a side-angle. Danny shook his head, "No, Jack. I want the *immediacy,* the *impact* of a full, front-on shot."

"But Danny, that water will be coming straight at you."

"Hey, you gotta *be a man*, Jack. It's a once-in-a-lifetime shot. What am I gonna do, miss it?"

"But Danny--"

And then Jimmy Shorty was at my side, pulling me away. "Jackson, we need you over here. Seems like we got a little problem..." We walked over to his battered old jeep, with him talking about the pleasantness of the day and the beauty of this particular part of the canyon. From where we were, I could still see Danny off in the distance, setting up his big wooden tripod directly in front of the pipe.

"Jimmy--", I interrupted, "Danny's setting up right in front of that pipe you warned us about."

He gave me a warm smile and a pat on the back, at the same time steering me further away from the rig. "He don't listen too good, does he, that Danny?" It was more a statement than a question.

"He doesn't listen *at all*, Jimmy."

"Me and the boys been seeing how he treats you and the rest of the crew. You know, a youngster like that has got to be taught to grow."

"We should just *let* him get hit with that water?"

Jimmy shrugged and nodded his head, "Yep. It's the kindest thing we could do for him. Don't you agree?"

"Well...let's at least go back so we can pick up the pieces."

By the time we returned, Danny was ragging at Jim Sam, one of the operators, "Damn it, now be sure you have enough water pressure! I want this to be spectacular!"

Jim's grin was enormous, "Oh, she'll be a gusher, all right. You jist tell me when you want it, that there will be our signal."

Danny pulled a handkerchief from his pocket, "I'll yell, *and* I'll wave my red bandanna, to be sure there's no screwup."

The grin faded from Jim Sam's face. Danny's meaning was clear, he had to be sure Jim Sam didn't screw up. I saw Jim fiddling with some dials, and the water pressure seemed to shoot up another few notches, near the top of the reading.

I looked at my friend, "Jimmy, are you sure--?"

"Jackson, you sure-fire do worry too much. It's the result of too much of that fast-paced city living."

I checked all the cameras and yelled to Danny, "Okay, then, if you're sure you want to do this."

"God DAMN it, Jack, let's GO!"

"Okay," I sighed. I checked the two camera positions. Both cameramen were watching me, waiting for my signal, "Cameras will roll on my call. Be ready. Here we go...3-2-1...ACTION!"

My cameraman nodded and grunted, "Rolling."

The second cameraman yelled from high in the rig, "Rolling."

Danny had a momentary problem--he'd forgotten to take off the safety, and then he too said, "Rolling!" A moment went by and nothing happened. "Damn it, I said ROLLING!" he shouted.

"Wave the bandanna, Danny," I yelled at him. "Your signal, remember?"

Danny had totally lost his cool, as they used to say in those days. Red-faced, he threw his bandanna in the air and screamed, "LET ME HAVE IT, YOU GODDAM SAVAGE!"

Jim Sam's unholy grin was a sight to see.

"Yes sir, boss!" he said, pulling hard on a huge lever.

One shaft of water shot 80 feet in the air, bathing the cameraman hanging high in the rig. The second stream boiled out of the 8-inch pipe, lifting Danny off his feet and sending him flying backward through the air. Danny hit the ground hard 15 feet from where he'd taken off and rolled ass-over-teakettle down a small hill, and ended up sputtering and red-faced in a clump of cactus.

The Indian crew was beside themselves, rolling on the ground and laughing so hard, tears were coming to their eyes and they couldn't catch their breath. And, God help me, I was laughing, too. The thought kept going through my mind, *The Navajos water the desert...with laughter.* We managed to calm down enough to get Danny out of the cactus. Getting the cactus out of Danny took much longer, but we finally headed back to the motel.

Young Danny held on to as much of his dignity as he could by assuring us that he'd gotten the "topper" shot that would make our film great, but we never did find out, because the water and the hard fall cracked the magazine and destroyed the film.

I've been on countless sets since then, doing all sorts of things--writer, assistant director, director, producer, publicity writer, and so on--and, Hollywood being the self-important and foolish place it is, there have been times when things have gotten outrageous and nearly unbearable. When that happens, I try to remember my good friends, the Navajos, and the lesson they taught me. *We are all together in this world...no celebrity, no filmmaker, no star, no shot is so important that a man should treat the people under him with less than the dignity and respect that they deserve.*

The Death of the Mole-Digger

Now, as far back as my college days, I had a Navajo friend that I probably didn't deserve. His name was Jim Shorty, and he had a keen eye for people, a slow way of talking, and a twinkle in his eye that I rarely understood. He was working for a degree in geology, and--believe it or not--he was one of the first Navajos ever to get a college degree. Back in those days I didn't really have time for friends or friendship; it was very low on my scale of importance. I was on my way somewhere. Jimmy, seeing that I was a young fellow with little or no time for humor and that I spent my days burrowing after all manner of relatively unimportant things in an intense sort of way, gave me the nickname Mole-digger.

When I was first banging away at the typewriter, even before I was getting paid for it, I never made this connection, that I was digging in a very narrow tunnel toward objectives that might not be as universal as I myself had decided. Like many young writers, I used to think what I did was high art, and very complicated. Only I could "get it". Not only was there just this one right way; somehow, because of the unique and amazing person that I was, through sheer concentration I alone could ferret out these deep, hidden secrets and somehow bring them to light. And so, in this manner, I would finally create that mythic holy grail of all our youth who choose the way of the scribe--I would write The Great American Novel.

Now even today I don't claim that I understand Southwestern Indians...but it has come to my attention that one of the pleasures of the Navajo mind is its delight in ambiguity. Back then, I was never sure if I was "the mole who digs", or "the one who digs for moles". But I'm pretty sure that, if you had seen me in those early days, squinting over a thick science book behind my coke-bottle thick glasses, you'd have realized that either definition would have applied. I wasn't interested in that. I thought my problem was that lousy name. I didn't want anything to do with it. If I had to have a damn Indian appellation, why couldn't I be Fierce-Warrior, Strong-As-Bull, Knife-Mind or Graceful-Runner? Why did I have to be The-One-Who-Digs-For-Moles?

Back then, there was no answer to the question. I would ask Jimmy what it meant and why he had given it to me and he would just shrug and give me that sly grin of his. "It is you, Jackson," he would say. "You *are* the Mole-Digger."

I went away to grad school and Vietnam, and he served in Germany and ended up *back on the rez*, as they say, as the head of a Navajo team that drilled the Four Corners area looking for water. He had an interesting way of life, I thought, and so one day when I was looking for new projects, I asked Jimmy if I could write a short documentary about him and what he did. "Why shore!," he said enthusiastically, his voice filled with enthusiasm and amusement. "Does this mean you're a-comin' out this way to see us?"

I sent 20 or so pages away to a guy named Danny who ran the educational department of a major Hollywood film company, and he bought it straightaway. Not only that, Danny was so impressed with the fresh new EMMY award I'd won that he wanted me to direct.

Easy pickings, I thought, and said I had an opening in my schedule and would be glad to do it.

I was used to working more or less alone, shooting my own stuff, picking up the sound wild and then syncing it in later. But Danny decided a couple of weeks on the reservation would be a grand time, and so he would come along. That meant he had to bring Patty, his pretty Japanese secretary, and a bunch of other people.

Danny was barely 20, but he was very self-confident. He said he'd decided I should spend my time directing, so he hired me a really great Austrian cameraman, who needed an assistant as well to load the film magazines and keep the sand from gumming up his cameras. But then, sometime before we left, Danny hired a second cameraman, so he'd have one of his own. Dueling cameramen...I had the uneasy feeling we were competing.

We showed up in Window Rock driving three production vehicles--a hot Ford Bronco with big sand tires and a camera mount screwed to the top of the heavy black roll bar, a brand new blue Toyota Land Cruiser that was on loan from Samuelson Publicity in return for film credits, and a battered old English Land Rover that looked like it had already lost a battle with several rhinos and elephants.

Jim Shorty looked at us as we piled out of our production cars. When I introduced Danny as the boss, Shorty could hardly contain his delight. Danny was ten years younger than we were, with the pimply, round face of a high school sophomore. He had the *Hollywood Attitude*, and must have seemed very brash to these Southwesterners, the way he *pushed* to have his way in everything. I thought Shorty would be offended, but he didn't say anything and his grin got wider and wider as he watched Danny running around bossing things. Jimmy introduced us to his crew, Sammy Lee and Jim Sam, two tough-as-leather Indians who drove and operated the huge water-drilling rig. Jimmy introduced

Danny as the boss, and *all* the Indians grinned at young Danny, and then we went off to dinner.

The Navajos Water the Desert was the first film I'd directed from a script that was longer than a commercial. It was a shock to me, because I had to start to think like a film person, figuring things out in terms of angles, cuts, closeness and impact of objects and action on the screen, and the continuity involved in pure storytelling. And everywhere I went, Danny was right next to me, setting up a complementary or competing angle, making sure *I had it covered*.

He *was* a fierce competitor, and before long he was joking about how much better shape he was in than I was. A big event in life back then was the 30-year mark, and I was already past it, *over the hill*, as he taunted. So I accepted a challenge that, if we finished our filming on the next day, I would race him up a boulder-strewn slope to the top of a butte that he pointed out.

That night some strange things happened that I can only guess at. We had, at Jimmy's request, snuck a few cases of beer onto the reservation. I'd gone to bed early, determined to be in the best possible shape to run up the hill and beat Danny. While I was sleeping, the crew and our Navajo friends had gotten happy around the swimming pool. There had been some sort of emotional triangle between one of the cameramen, Danny, and his secretary Patty. The next morning, Danny showed up on the set looking puffy-eyed and combative. It was one of those days when the mood of the crew was intense and picky. Angry comments flew around, bruised feelings didn't begin to mend, and through it all, Jimmy and his two workers smiled and went about their jobs as the main actors in our film.

We finished our final shot for the day and wrapped the set just as the red-gold sun set over the butte we had to climb. Seeing as it was a little later than I had expected, and I wasn't all that thrilled at the prospect of jogging up a snake-infested hillside, I was willing to call off the race, but Danny wouldn't hear anything of it. His youthful features were set into his *grim and determined* look; he looked like a pouting kid. *Oh great,* I thought, *He doesn't get laid and he has to take it out on me.* He went over to the Toyota and started to change into his sneakers. The Land Cruiser now sported a bent fender from a cow Danny'd hit while high-speeding along the road from Gallup on the previous night. It was another thing he didn't want to talk about.

I walked over to the Bronco and started to put on my own lighter-weight shoes. Jimmy came and sat on the hood of the Bronco. "You know," he said casually, "It's come to my mind that it ain't really how fast a person goes up that hill, it's probably picking the right trail before you start."

"That so?" I said.

"Now a fresh young guy like Danny is likely to want to go straight up. But if it was *me,* bein' over 30 and all and having the accumulated wisdom of those extra ten years, I think I'd kinda go up slant-wise."

"You would, huh?"

"Yup. I would. See that faint trail like maybe some antelope or a cow or something used it a couple of times?" I followed the way he was pointing.

"You think it's fair to be telling me this?"

"I tried to point it out to Danny, but he don't listen much."

"You knew he wouldn't listen."

"Jackson, you old Mole-Digger, *Whut* are you talking about?!" He clapped me on the back and burst into laughter. "Anyway, me and the boys," he indicated Jim Sam and Sammy Lee, "we kinda put a bet on you."

"I hope I don't let you down."

Danny and I agreed to start right from the Toyota. First man to the top would wave his shirt. The Indians and the crew would have two sets of binoculars, and would agree on the winner. As an extra touch, Danny insisted we each carry one of the two-way walkie-talkies we used to communicate for the long-range shots. He said it was for safety, but from the way he grinned at me, I knew he was thinking the extra weight would be the touch that would drag me down to defeat. I shrugged as if it didn't matter and took the walkie-talkie.

That's when Danny dropped the final bombshell, "Patty is coming, too. She'll go along with me."

"I thought she didn't like heights. She was talking about it at dinner the other night."

"Nonsense," Danny laughed. "Being afraid of heights or anything else is just a state of mind."

"That hill is no place to find out."

"You afraid you're going to get beaten *by the both of us?*"

I ignored him, talking to Patty, "Is this your idea?"

"I really *want* to go," she said. But she looked troubled, and I wondered what part of the previous night's misadventures was still being played out.

Jimmy drawled, "Three, Two, One--GO!", and Danny tore away from us, heading straight up the hill with Patty right behind him. She was in great shape, probably in as good shape as he was. I could have just stood there and watched her go, but there was work to be done. I tossed Jimmy a little salute and started on a fast trot diagonal to the mountain to pick up the faint trail he'd pointed out. The walkie-talkie was banging against my thigh, and so I unclipped it and carried it in my hand, alternating back and forth when I got tired.

After a hundred feet, the slope started to slant upward at a stiffer angle, and as I made my first cut-back, I had to dodge some bowling ball sized rocks dislodged from above. Danny and Patty were about 150 feet above me, still heading straight for the top, but they were now on the talus part of the slope, and slipping halfway back for every foot they gained.

There was still plenty of afterglow, but the sun was now well beyond the horizon and the light was beginning to fade. I ran on, mopping the sweat from my forehead and scrambling a bit to keep my footing on the narrow pathway. I was about 300 feet up the slope, halfway through the talus. Danny and Patty had gained another 50 feet on me, and had reached the top of the talus slope. They couldn't go straight up anymore, but would have to move from outcropping to outcropping, using handholds to keep from slipping on the crumbly sandstone. I saw them head off along a fairly steep little ridge that seemed to disappear into a small area of shrubs. I should be steadily catching up from now on. I took my third switchback. In the dimming light, I had to pick my way carefully, placing my feet from rock to rock. Danny and Patty were no longer in sight. A cool breeze had started up, and I trotted on, feeling fairly confident.

Suddenly my radio squawked, "Base to Danny. Base to Danny. Are you having difficulty?" There was no reply, and the call was repeated over and over.

I took the next switchback, and as I started back to my left across the slope, a huge boulder bounded about 40 feet in front of me. My radio squawked, "Base to Mole-Digger. Jackson, Jackson, come in, Jackson."

I slowed to a walk and pressed the talk button, "What, Jimmy?"

"Danny has left Patty at an outcropping about 30 yards up and to your left. Can you see her?"

"No. She must be behind the brush."

He didn't say anything more, and I continued running. I was gasping for air now, regretting all those after-work beers I'd shared with the gang over the last few years. I came to another switchback in the trail--and saw Patty. She was on a very steep part of the slope, gripping one lone outcrop like it was her lover. I could see Danny straight above her, churning relentlessly toward his goal. He wasn't making much headway against the mountain, and if I really pushed it, I could overtake him in the next few minutes. But I would have to leave Patty and continue along my own trail.

I yelled to her, but she ignored me. There was a shower of rocks from above and for a moment she disappeared from sight in a cloud of dust. I twitched the call-button, "Jimmy, she looks frozen. I don't think she's hurt, but I gotta go get her."

There was no response. I moved away from the trail and started to angle up the loose gravel slope toward her. It took several minutes, and I arrived in a positive hail of rocks from above. It took several minutes to calm Patty and to convince her to let go of the outcropping. She'd been hit by a rock and had a small dribble of blood running from her hair. I daubed at it, and told her everything was going to be fine, but we had to go, *now and together*, or she wouldn't get down before dark. I asked her if she wanted to spend the night on the mountain. Her eyes widened, and she shook her head no. I took her hand and we both half-slid back the way I had come. It was touch-and-go for a few minutes, mostly because she was so frightened I had to place her hands and feet on the safe places and the handholds. We both started to slip a time or two, and when we finally got back to the original path I'd been taking, we were both sweaty and shaking. I thumbed the walkie-talkie, "I've got her back to the trail, Jimmy. Not much light anymore, but I think we'll be okay. See you in five minutes."

There was a moment's pause, and then the walkie-talkie crackled one more time. "Good work," the voice drawled from the crackly little speaker. "You done real good, Mountain Eagle."

The Cowboy & the Little Blue People

Good timing's everything, you know, whether it's seducing the sweet young art director down the hall or selling your latest creative idea to The Big Dude upstairs. When your timing is right, you're on greased skids to heaven...or hell, as it were, the basic rule being never mess around in your own office, and if you're married, never mess around at all. At least, that's the rule.

Now when I was in Saigon I wanted to learn French very badly, so as I generally tried to take a half-day off from the war anyway, I enrolled in French 101 at *L'Ecole Francaise*. In between learning phrases like "shut up" and "I don't know" (the French feelings toward *les Americaines* in South East Asia during this period wobbled between disdain and disgust), I was encouraged to take out a subscription to a Belgian comic book called <u>Spirou</u>. This bright weekly magazine interspersed informational articles on the newest Peogeots, Alfa Romeos and Mirage fighters between games, puzzles, inventions, camping and science stories, and comic strips. On one of the pages you might find "Mangeurs D'Hommes", a story on sharks. And "Sur Tous Les Fronts Du Sports", a quick sports update. The comic strips ranged from the quirky "Gaston Lagaffe" to the serious adventures of "Mark

Dacier". There were "Les Plus Belles Histoires De L'Oncle Paul" and "Les Aventures Du Capitaine Morgan", "La Ribambelle" and many others. Ever a sucker for a comic, I also was being enlightened, picking up enough street-French to make my way around the better bars and bordellos of the Mekong Delta.

Five years later I found myself back in L.A. working as a nonunion writer/producer for Hanna-Barbera, home of the legendary Flintstones, that loveable scamp-dog Scooby-Doo and the weird and wacky Banana Splits (in case you've never slipped on the Banana Splits, they were fur-suited derivatives of the Monkeys, who were themselves derivatives of the Beatles). By this time, Bill Hanna and Joe Barbera were already treasured bits of Hollywood history. They'd directed Tom & Jerry cinema shorts at Warner Brothers in the olden days (the early 50's), and pioneered low-budget animation for television when theatrical cartoons went the way of the *Tyrannosaurus Rex*. When this happened, Bill and Joe shifted gears so well they soon became the kings of Saturday morning kid shows.

I was restless with my assignments in their industrial and educational departments, and started moonlighting the shop, racking my brains as a new show developer for Joe. It was no big deal, being a show developer for Joe. He was a truly voracious idea-eater; if you had fresh thinking, he wanted you for breakfast, and half the people working in Hollywood today used to be new show developers for Joe at one time or another.

I don't mean it was bad, or that he was a bad guy. He wasn't. Joe treated you like a person (rather than a serf, which is the more common Hollywood attitude). He had a charming, wolf-like smile and was the only man I'd ever met with blue-black hair, just like a cartoon pirate. And anyone could learn a lot from Joe. He was a *master salesman*, he could sell you your own shoes and get you to give back change. I was there once when the projector broke down during a major presentation to

ABC for the next year's programming; the room went black as pitch and Joe used the time *to wing it off-the-cuff and sell some kid's horror show that was totally unrelated to the original presentation, a "little something he'd just had on the back of his mind for a while"*.

At any rate, this was 1969 and all the Saturday morning cartoon guys were being hammered by the educational clique to develop uplifting learning experiences that proposed to teach the youth of America to live harmoniously together in one big, happy family. A bitter pill for Bill and Joe, who by nature ran the river with Huck Finn and flew, dove or drove along with Tom Swift's latest invention. I can hear their outrage yet today...*When Tom hit Jerry with the mallet or blew him up, it's <u>fun</u>, fer Christ-sake! Kids <u>need</u> action and adventure, things to get them away from all that deadly dull stuff being drummed in their heads! Gee-mon-eezis, they get enough of that at <u>school</u>! Entertain 'em <u>first</u>-- this ain't supposed to be lousy <u>homework</u>! It's <u>competition</u> that makes America unique--what have we got here, a bunch of panty-waisted <u>commies</u>?!*

Though they both resented to the marrow of their bones what they saw as "soft" shows being shoved down their throats, Joe was a touch more omnivorous than Bill, recognizing that his prime job was to stuff the maws of the petty, fierce and pampered monster that Saturday Morning had become. Thus it is, the beast begins to shape its master.

That's why Joe was more or less open to the untried when I cut up about 20 or 30 of my old <u>Spirou</u> magazines and mounted various strange and exotic European story ideas in a big presentation and called him and Bill into the conference room. My idea was, the guys over in Brussels had already developed this great pool of stuff, and all we had to do was tap in. Joe seemed to like that. I remember some of the things I pasted up: There was "Max l'Exploreur" (a hip and confident little colonial who confronted savage perils in darkest Africa), "Lucky Luke" (a drool, laconic cowpoke who got it off talking things over with his horse, Jolly Jumper) and "The Smurfs" (a friendly soapy concerning the lives and troubles of the peaceful little blue people who lived in the woods).

I remember doing this presentation with Bill snarling "soft, *soft*..." under his breath the entire time like he was drawing himself as the growly mutt in one of his own cartoons. Not a good sign. Still, everybody was fittingly impressed with the amount of work that went into the pitch, bla-bla-bla...but in the end it was no sale. I stuck the Spirou presentation in the bag called "experience", and went on to other things.

A few years later I was running a TV commercial production company and commuting weekly between L.A., Detroit and New York when I heard Bill & Joe had contacted the Belgians about running "The Smurfs" as a summer replacement. Since my presentation (I didn't say *because* of it), some top European artists had seen the same potential and had gotten down to their animation boards, and the good people of Spirou had a bunch of Smurfs in the can, ready to run on the air waves. All H-B had to do was strip the French dialogue from the shows and redo them in English. They could even mix sound from the original M&E (music & effects) track. Well, the show caught on, and there were little blue people all over America.

The point is, it took an open slot in one of the network schedules and a batch of wonderfully written and already-produced shows to convince those two legendary cartoon men to reluctantly give one of the most successful and long-running cartoon series ever created the chance to take off from the runway.

Hey, you think they should have known better? You wish it were so simple, being a Living Legend. Joe also gave "Lucky Luke" a shot, but it died a horrible and unhappy death. There's something vaguely amusing about an Old West cowboy, American as apple pie, shouting "*Formez le cercle! Lachez les betes!*" But it somehow loses itself in the translation. (Form a circle! Tie down the animals!) You see it, don't you? *Anybody* can see that...in retrospect. But sometimes, even when you're at the top of your game, you have to *do it*, to pour the whole pile of nickels down the drain, just to figure out something that simple, *that it doesn't work.*

All I can say is, as you prepare your next surefire winner of an idea for presentation, remember your success or failure will hinge on shifts of the social winds and complexities of individual human subjectivity beyond your wildest ken. So stir the entrails of topical culture (some call it pop) and study the people you're selling to. And then go at your pitch with careful plotting, an exacting game plan, consummate salesmanship and unrelenting perseverance...and *then* hope for a little luck somewhere along the way. After you make the sale and become a legend in your own right, after your show's been running for six or seven years and you've paid off the home in the Bahamas, *then* you can shrug and give the reporter from <u>Variety</u> a vague little smile and call it good timing.

HARD SELL

It was the early 70's and it was just past noon on a day in February, a terrific breezy blue-sky Southern California winter day. At this time I was Head of Broadcast Production for Grey/Detroit. There was ankle deep slush back in Motor City, but I was in L.A. for at least another week.

I swung my cherry red, rented boss Mustang convertible into the small parking lot at Dove Films. They were casting for a Coke commercial and the lot was swarming with dozens of all-American beauties-- great legs, great faces, great bodies stuffed in tight shorts and t-shirts, and they parted in smiling flocks as I gunned the big V-8 into the vacant spot marked CLIENT.

The lobby, too, was overflowing with pretty girls. *What a job these Hollywood Moguls had!* Jim Ramsey, the Grey Creative Director and our head writer on the Ford Account, poked his head out of a doorway and waved a handful of typewritten pages, "Client Approval!"

I grinned and made my way toward him. It looked like the final hurtle had been jumped, we had an absolute green light to do the spots.

Jim grinned back, "And I've made reservations at Musso Franks for tonight!"

It was a Grey ritual, when we got a big approval we all gathered around a noisy, crowded table at Musso Franks for hot sourdough bread, steamed clams and many rounds of Heineken beer. I raised my hands to the imaginary god of advertising creatives and sang out happily, "Troi, Dut, Nuoc, Oiii!", which loosely translated means, "Sky, Earth, Water, Everything!"

Our director, Haskell Wexler, stuck his head out of one of the other offices to see what the noise was all about. He had a lean, aesthetic look and a deceptively mild manner, "What on earth was that you're saying?"

"Vietnamese," I said, wondering why I had blurted that out in the first place.

He perked up right away, "You speak Vietnamese?"

"Well, I used to. Forty-seven weeks at the Defense Language Institute in Monterey and a year in Saigon. I guess I learned something."

He motioned to the people in the room to wait for him, and took me by the arm, walking a little ways down the hall to where we could talk alone, "Beautiful! What a coincidence! Look, I'd really like you to come and see this film tonight."

I'd only met Haskell a few days before, but he was an established Hollywood person, and I was flattered. *Heck, I could have steamers any time.*

"Well, sure", I said. "What kind of film?"

"Documentary on Vietnam. Beautiful footage. Shot by some Scandinavians. You'll love it."

I had momentary misgivings. It had been years since I'd been in Vietnam, "I won't be asked to translate, will I...?"

He shook his head. "No, of course not. I'd just like to get your opinion on the film. It's got a Scandinavian narration track, but we've got a translator coming to handle it." He gave me a conspiratorial wink, "And I want you to meet some special friends of mine...Deal?"

I took his extended hand, "Deal."

I pulled the boss Mustang into a parking spot on the street as close as I could get to USC, glad for once that it was just a rented car. I don't know if you know that neighborhood, but it's over near Watts. It didn't look too safe to me, with graffiti scrawled on every available wall, and teenage kids looking at the car like it was treasure for pillage.

The room was fairly small, and stuffy. Ten or fifteen scruffy film students sat around a long table on which rested a projector. A white screen was set up across the room. The kids mostly had hair down to their jackets, and beards serious as they could grow them. The preferred garment was faded army fatigues. I knew how hot and uncomfortable fatigues were; it was stuff I hadn't worn since the day I got out of the service. There were a lot of "V for Victory" anti-war buttons and neck chain pendants with the drooping triangle peace symbol.

More students trickled in while I was being introduced, until the place was packed four deep back to the walls. Haskell made up a couple things about how fluent in Vietnamese I was. My face got red, and the worried note crept back in my mind. I didn't see anybody around that looked like a European Interpreter.

The film was set up on a dual projection system. It was 16 millimeter interlock, a system that's uncommon in the advertising business, but is used quite frequently by documentary filmmakers and students because 16 is cheaper than 35, and because you can show a picture around to try and sell it without taking it back to the lab for added expense of a finished answer print.

Fifteen minutes went by, and everybody just sat there. Nobody got impatient; in fact, there was an expectant air in the room. And then the door opened and there was a great flurry of welcomes and cheers--and in walked Tom Hayden and Jane Fonda!

I guess you know Jane from all the movies she's starred in, and you probably remember the controversy she stirred up when she went to Hanoi and was photographed in a flak helmet, peering up into the sky with a gun crew on the lookout for invading Gangster-American fighter-bombers, a picture with which Communist propagandists the world over had their field day. Tom Hayden, her husband back then, was a famous radical himself, very influential in the anti-war movement.

I was really surprised. I didn't know what to think. I stared at Jane, and all I could think was that she was a lot shorter than I'd imagined. Then somebody snapped the lights off and the room full of scruffy students disappeared. The projector disappeared. Even Tom and Jane disappeared. To say it simply, the film was WONDERFUL...but I didn't love it.

For the first time in seven years, I was back with the people I had tried so hard to help. I could smell the rich earth of the delta, the salty smell of gunpowder, feel again the muggy blasts of late spring heat and the thick rains of the wet, taste the pho and the nuoc man and the Beef Seven Ways, share again the fun and the tinny music and the bargirl laughter, hear the heavy saw of Brownings and the PAM of the M-1s, relive the stark moments when the flares drifted down and we all wondered if the sappers would get through this time...once again the heartaches, the hopes, the agony, the screams, the horror.

The interpreter didn't show up that night, but it wouldn't have mattered, because the Scandinavian narration track was missing anyway. What they did have was a background track that was about 95% lip-sync Vietnamese. And the entire roomful of people turned to me, expecting me to tell them what was going on.

Part of me wanted to help, but it just wasn't possible. I had cauterized that part of my brain years ago, so I wouldn't bleed to death. I felt numb, encased in ice. The students all wanted to know what was going on. What are the Vietnamese saying, saying, saying...? I just shook my head, my tongue frozen, brain frozen, emotions frozen. It wasn't an empathetic time in our country; there was no way these people could understand what was going on inside my head, and no way I could tell them. Pretty soon I was getting dirty looks, the students figuring I was CIA or some other government spy dropped in their midst. I wondered what they would think if they knew I had been in the top secret National Security Agency, or that I'd had a Top Secret Codeword classification.

The picture flickered to an end. The lights came on, and Haskell was looking at me like I was a traitor, like I'd sold out my own country. He turned to Tom and Jane, making his silent apologies. I suppose I should have been angry, should have stood on the table and shouted that they all didn't know shit, that I'd studied the whole thing, that I'd gone to Vietnam and seen what it really was like, that the Vietnamese were good people, great people, and that they deserved to be helped by us, to be saved from communist domination. But I didn't. I couldn't.

You see, I was boxed in. The entire, subtle web of propaganda half-truths, just as effective as anything I could say about a Ford or a Schlitz or a Marlboro, had me pinned like a bug on the wall. I was just another poisonous creature labeled Invader-Gangster. Invader-Gangster American. Colonialist Pig American. Nguoi My Sao, Ugly American. Number Ten, Ugly American. Inside, where I all too infrequently thought about values like honor and giving one's word, I felt broken and crushed; but even then, as a professional, I had to tip my hat to the other side--THAT was GREAT advertising.

Nobody said anything much, and the meeting broke up quickly, everybody thinking about hidden cameras and microphones. I made my way alone through the Watts streets, walking back to the Mustang. A few young blacks were sitting on the hood talking their jive talk, but nobody'd swiped anything, and so I got in and drove away. It wasn't too late; I could still make it down to Musso Franks for the last round of steamers and beers. But I didn't feel like it.

On Bowing to Royalty

Since I've seen Helen Mirren's Oscar-winning performance in <u>The Queen</u>, I've had a little more tolerance for royalty. Not much, but a little. There was a time when I didn't have any at all.

In part, I think, my bad attitude stems from that time my father took me aside to explain how there would always be someone bigger, richer, tougher and smarter than myself. In part, I say, because he must have seen a problematic something in my character to cause him to say such things in the first place.

Like a lot of workingmen who had lived through the Great Depression, my dad was always on the defensive. Life was out to get you, and sooner or later it would. An isolationist and an America-firster, he nonetheless despised the Nazis, and tried to join up and fight in World War II. The army turned him down because he'd lost most of the fingers from one of his hands in a stamping mill accident. He also didn't like Ford motorcars, because he thought Henry Ford (one of America's first peaceniks) was soft on Nazis.

By the time WWII was over, Old Henry's hands were no longer on the wheel, and his grandson, Henry II (known among the Motor City insiders as *The Deuce*) had to fight to regain control of the company for the family. Once he was back in the driver's seat, the younger Ford drove them to new heights and the company regained its luster. Of course, these days with the invasion of the Asian motor companies, Ford's future is cloudy, but in the 1970's Henry II was every bit as powerful as the old man.

When I worked at Grey/Detroit on the Ford Corporate account, everybody was whispering about the autocratic way he'd dismissed his chief rival, Lee Iacocca. Lee had been responsible for developing the Mustang and several other popular Ford cars, and felt he was the natural heir to the Ford throne. One day, without any advance warning, Henry II told Lee he had to go. When the stunned Iacocca asked, "Why, Henry, Why?!", *The Deuce* had simply replied, "Because, Lee, I don't like you."

In those days, it seemed to me Henry II was the closest thing to royalty you could find in this country. At the snap of his fingers, he could command, hire or fire thousands of employees. His word and wishes were as law in Detroit, a mean serf-town where the various races lived in ethnic pockets--Greek, Jewish, Polish, Blacks-- with the large black population trapped in the meanest slums of all.

I don't know how to explain the mutual affection that came to exist between *The Deuce* and Lord Louis Mountbatten, son of Prince Louis Alexander and related to most European royalty. Lord Mountbatten had directed allied forces in Southeast Asia in WWII, mostly in Burma, and, as such, had done his bit to crush the very Nazis with whom Old Man Henry was said to want to live in peace and harmony.

I was Head of Commercial Production on the Ford Corporate account when Lord Mountbatten came to Motor City to put the squeeze on his rich American friend. The Lord, having enjoyed a full and rich existence, had put his life into a dull and deadly seven-hour documentary. When I heard he was coming, I looked him up in the 1959 World Book Encyclopedia, and I didn't see how anybody could squeeze seven hours out of that life.

The real story: Although born of royalty, His Lordship had served in the British navy as a common sailor in World War I. By WWII, he was in command of the British destroyer Kelly when it was ingloriously sunk. With his connections, he was given another ship and allowed to scuttle around in covert operations near Nazi-occupied France for a while, and finally sent to faraway Burma where for the duration he wasn't in command of anything else that sank. After that, he was Viceroy of India, supervising its collapse into Pakistan and India, and, again, while one is tempted to blame him for it, there is no evidence to indicate he was any more than secondarily involved. He returned to sea duty as a chief of supplies and transport, was promoted to 1st Sea Lord and finally, in 1956, to Admiral of the Fleet. If you've heard Gilbert & Sullivan's bright and witty lyrics, "I am the ruler of the Queen's Navy," you've got the picture.

Anyway, knowing that Ford was committed to programming that "mattered to society" (instead of the usual trashy television fare), His Lordship felt there was a good chance he could hit up Henry II to get the entire miserable seven hours on the small screen in front of the American people so they could see for themselves that for which they should be properly grateful.

Cornered like Scrooge McDuck in his own vault, *The Deuce* coughed up enough scratch to run one hour. It wasn't *the whole incredible life,* but on the other hand 60 minutes on network television in the United States wasn't chopped liver, either. So His Lordship breezed into town to record this latest of his historic moments, just in case he lived long enough to bless the world with an eighth hour of footage on his remarkable life.

At this time, somebody somewhere in the pecking order of things out at the Glass House--which is what we called the Ford Headquarters building in Dearborn--

decided that the great motor company's in-house film department would do the shoot. My bosses at Grey Advertising, recognizing the somewhat limited capabilities of Ford's in-house shutterbugs, ordered me to be there to make sure they didn't trip over their shoelaces. After some hemming and hawing to make sure I wouldn't be scabbing (the in-house group was non-union, whereas I belonged to the Directors Guild), I agreed to lend what weight I could on the side of reason and light, strictly as a sidelines consultant.

When I got out to the Glass House, the setup looked okay. They had multiple cameras at every position to cover themselves in case the film should go bad or lightning strike a member of the crew, and they were placed appropriately. The lighting looked okay and everybody seemed in focus. None of the listless swines were drinking on the set, at least that I could see. That was about all I could do. And since the non-guild director was looking at me like I was dog poop, I thought I'd go stand in the shadows by the rear exit and see if he could say "action" while chewing gum at the same time.

And then Henry II and Lord Batty showed up. It is hard to describe the sense of power I felt as *The Deuce* entered the room. It was as if there was a strong gale moving with his presence. I imagined the room swayed and grown men were near to fainting. I realized how much I really didn't want to be there. The image of a cartoon comic strip character from my youth came to my mind. It was the entrance of Henry the Chicken Hawk, all full of bustle and self-importance. There it was, my bad attitude. Why couldn't I ever, just once, get along with the others like all the happy little critters on Sesame Street?

And if you think the room stirred when Henry II strutted in, you should have seen the entrance of His Lordship. He was haughty and grim-faced. His look and posture reminded me of General Douglas MacArthur's skinny older brother (if he had one). One look around the room and I could see everybody--crew, PR flacks, agency people--everybody was glassy-eyed. Now the invisible winds of power were pushing normally rational minds around like feathers in a storm. This was a flock of men ready to pee in their pants. I was looking at real magic.

I remember taking it all well enough until one of the account guys told us to get ready to kneel. That made me blink; I hadn't knelt since my last boyhood confession, and I hadn't liked it then.

"Kneel?!" I whispered. "For whom? Henry or Batty?"

"For His Lordship!" he shot back angrily. "It's English custom. Get ready. Here they come!"

"Isn't that old custom just for the Queen?"

"God DAMN it, Klawitter...get DOWN!"

"Sorry, guy," I said. "This just isn't my sort of thing."

I winked and gave him a little salute and quietly slid out the back door. The last glimpse I had of the sordid affair was of a line of perfectly normal advertising executives in their best suits getting down on their knees. Somehow that seemed appropriate.

Another minute and I was in my feisty little turf-brown Bronco truck, headed back to the agency. Sure, I'd never be able to write on my resume that I'd directed Henry II or Lord Mountbatten. On the other hand, they'd never be able to say that they'd directed me.

It's Who You Know

If Jon Peters had done Olga Wolinski's hair instead of Barbra Streisand's, would he be a big-shot Hollywood dude today? Maybe. And maybe not. Of course, in a town where every hairdresser has a script tucked away among the curlers, that's probably an unfair question. Still, I wonder how he approached that whole thing, *Uhh, Barbra darling, I got this script here...* Naaa, he probably found a more dignified approach, *Barbie-love, did you ever stop to think <u>hairstyling</u> actually has a good bit of <u>dramatics</u> to it...?* Or maybe he went historical, *Gosh, Babs, did you know Mozart's barber actually wrote operas!?*

I see the next scene very clearly in my mind's eye: It's a week later and there's to be a very big meeting in this oak-paneled conference room with the stuffy heads of production, story, and the studio top pickle himself standing in. There's also an "A" writer (in show biz they grade writers like beef) and a very big director and a couple of agents wearing silk power ties. They've all been sitting around huffing and puffing and they've finally agreed on their next big project, by God! Now they're just waiting for the last sign-off, a formality, really. They tap their polished nails on the huge mahogany table and idly glance at their Omegas, aware of other things and other places. Suddenly the door bangs open and Barbra comes striding in, gorgeous and powerful in her new flip-tip haircut. Before anyone can say how radiant she looks, she flings a script on the center of the table. The pages have been curled by blow-dryers, and key passages are marked with hairpins. For a long moment, the men around the table are frozen in place, staring at the cover, which seems to have a little glob of mousse sliding down the side. "What's this?" someone finally has the nerve to ask.

A lot of Hollywood projects get their start because people *in the business* brush shoulders with people *who aren't*, at places like the corner 7-11, Chi Chi's Pizza and the local Chevron station. Last week a chauffeur who works for one of the studios told me he has a script in play based on his life as a gang-banger. Hey, I'm not knocking it--it happened to me once.

It was a half-lifetime ago, and I was new in Hollywood and green as grass (the lawn kind). I was over at my neighbor, Nikita Knatz's place, learning the Russian way to drink 100 proof vodka without getting plastered. With his secret methods handed down through his Russian heritage, Niki could hold a half gallon of the stuff; I was too schnockered to know whether it was working for me or not.

Even back then, the young Nikita--Niki, for short-- was a real Hollywood guy, a movie art director, storyboarder and artist. He'd trained under famous producer/director Norman Jewison on big pictures like Fiddler on the Roof. He had a great wrist, knew angles, lenses and cuts, and he could draw like lightning. Over the years since, he's worked on dozens and dozens of major pictures, and today he's as much in demand as ever--if you stick around after the movie's over, every once in a while you'll see his name on the credits. Or just IMDB him. His credits go on forever.

At that time, we lived next door to each other, and he was working with Steve McQueen, who had a three-picture deal (a three-pic pack, as they say) with CBS

Cinema Center. Niki had worked up three officially approved sketches of Steve (that means approved by Steve), and that was all he ever needed. He had a nearly front-on, a three-quarter, and a side shot, all of them from Steve's good side, and if he had to draw the great man looking the other way, he just flipped the sketch. As Steve's range of facial expression was fairly limited--from that familiar, grim little smile of his to the grim little frown that said *look out, mister*--Niki would just draw on the lips he wanted, Steve's flinty eyes and the rest of the lines on his face staying just about the same.

Beyond his craft, Nikita is a colorful guy in his own right. He's built like a diesel truck, with wide shoulders and the lower half of his broad face covered by a spade beard. You may even know his face. Early in his career he played in front of the camera--a character part in The Russians Are Coming and a couple of other things--and once in those Neanderthal times he was actually featured on the cover of Life Magazine as one of America's top up-and-coming young stars. He was tough, too--when he was a kid on the run from both the Russian commies and the Nazis, his mom dragged him halfway across Europe with a bullet in his stomach from a strafing Stukka, and he still has the huge scar to prove it. And, as if that wasn't enough, he'd been a pro footballer, as well, playing fourteen games for the old New York Titans, and he picked up a judo black belt from somewhere. Though he graduated from San Francisco State University, even today he speaks English like a thug from Brooklyn, enthusiastically, and without much emphasis on the diction.

Naturally, he was a Steve McQueen favorite. They used to ride bikes, drink, kick-box and in general knock around together, and on the set Niki had a second, unofficial role--he was the bouncer. People always seemed to be a little more polite to each other when he was looking on. Steve called him his leg-breaker. And because they got along so well, Niki had convinced

Steve to let him do the featurette of his next movie, which was slated to be a racing epic shot in Europe.

Now a featurette is a short film about the making of the movie. They went out of favor for a while, and are back in vogue today because DVDs have lots of space to stick extras on them, but back then featurette-making was a going business because the TV networks used them as fillers after first-run movies, which were of an odd length because they'd originally been produced for cinema release. Today the nets just cut the hell out of the movies to make them fit, but back then they didn't yet realize they could get away with that. Anyway, Niki had Steve's word that he could do the featurette, but he needed a "big idea" to convince the money boys at Cinema Center that he could do the job. That was where I came in.

I'd written, produced and directed commercials, industrials and documentaries by that time, but I'd never done a featurette. Still, with all that vodka inside me, it didn't seem too tough. We agreed I would come up with the idea and we would go partners. He gave me a couple of belts for the road and I staggered across the street to my place.

The next morning I sat on the patio overlooking Fredonia Street and a little piece of the Universal Studios lot, sat there with my hangover and my portable Olivetti on my lap. Thudding head and all, I wrote a single page about racing and how it felt to be a driver in one of the most dangerous races in the world. I'd never been in a race car in my life. It didn't seem important at the time...and, in a way, it still doesn't.

I described a scene where a racing driver is necking with a beautiful blond as he drives. They're cruising along in a convertible, the top is down, the moon is full. He's a thrill-seeker, and they go faster and faster. She laughs, throwing her head back in abandon, and he is drawn to the smooth curved skin of her neck. Just as he gives her a deep and powerful kiss, she clings to him and suddenly and horribly changes into a skeleton. "Le Mans is like that," I wrote. "Le Mans is a *French Kiss with Death*." I think I spilled coffee on the page, and got a little smear of orange marmalade on there too. It didn't matter; the money boys loved it.

Did I really know what I was doing? No, of course not. But a few months later I found myself in a first class seat on the Air France polar route, headed for Paris. And Niki and I did a featurette that both Steve and Gordon Stulberg, the head of Cinema Films, always said was one of the best they'd ever seen.

So, you see, you never know. The next time the kid who waits on you at Spago or Taco Bell shyly pulls out a sheaf of papers sticky with tomato sauce or salsa, maybe you better give him the time of day. You could be looking at your next big project.

Jonathan Williams' Lucky Walnut

Do you believe in magic? Luck? Fate? If you are going to be a successful professional creative person, you really have no other choice. Of course, it isn't easy, not these days with magic dying little by little every year. You've heard the theory--it's being replaced by science. Actually, that's not true. It's being killed by the pace of the world. By man out of harmony with his elements. And by bad storytelling.

On the other hand, magic still can be found anywhere and in anything, if you know how and where to look for it. Jonathan Williams found it in a walnut. He told me about it one sunny autumn afternoon in the Sarthe province of France, which is a lowland region of forests, farms and small villages not far from Paris where they run the French Grand Prix car race known as Le Mans.

Steve McQueen was living his dream, filming the high-speed rush he felt when he got behind the wheel of a racing car. I was a hot young documentary filmmaker, and I'd signed on to do a small film about "the making of the film", to create what is known in Hollywood show business as a *featurette*.

Mad Russian movie art director and genius Nikita Knatz, Jonathan and I were sitting by the side of the road near the end of the Mulsanne Straight, the exact place where there's a little bump and the cars go airborne and 80% of the drivers who are going to die at Le Mans take their mangle. We were waiting for second unit director Jack Reddish to reload so everybody could fire up the rubber tire beasts and do another run. That's the way it is in the movie business; a bit like the army-- hurry up and wait.

Jonathan was a professional racing driver, one of the few who looked enough the part so that he didn't need an actor double. We'd hired a bunch of them because McQueen was insisting on complete authenticity in his racing movie. That meant driving at or nearly at racing speeds. Jonathan raced on the Ferrari team, and he was the number three driver. He'd *always* been the number three driver, and that, he said, had been his problem.

The events he wanted to tell Nikita and me about took place three years before, which had to make it 1966 or 1967. At that time Jonathan was in his mid-twenties, and had been on the Italian team three years. As his fourth campaign began, the distressing pattern again made itself apparent. At Nuremburgring, where Ferrari came in 1-3-4, he took fourth place. At Le Mans, where *les belle rouges* came in 2-4-5, he took fifth.

They were in Monaco, thundering through the streets of that Mediterranean casino city when he decided he'd finally had enough of third. As the race spun around to the last lap, Jonathan's bright red car was in first place--except for the other two bright red cars driven by his teammates, which were in front of him. For the last five laps he had tried to get around the teammate directly in front of him--pushing high, pushing low, but always forced by time, space and mechanics to fall behind before the next turn. Was it the car itself? Was it his own lack of first place abilities? Was it simply fate and misfortune? There was no way to tell.

Regardless, he would get one more chance. He figured if he could go high in the short straightaway, he might just be able to squeeze in front of the second place car and drop back into the groove before the tunnel, which only accommodated single-lane traffic. But the straight itself wasn't long enough for this tricky maneuver, as everybody knew, and as he pulled out to pass, even he saw the seeming hopelessness of it all. There just wasn't enough of a stretch to accelerate, pull by and dip back into the groove before the side of the tunnel came up to smack you.

At this point, actions born of his months of frustration overtook Jonathan's normal reserve, and he calmly pushed the accelerator toward the floorboard. He could feel the roadside gravel under the tires, and he saw the number two driver look over and his eyes go wide as the number three car pulled even and the two of them raced side by side. There wasn't a person watching who thought Jonathan had a chance to make it. Even now, at this late and impossible moment, he might just barely save himself and his car by throttling back and cutting in behind the other car.

"And that was when," Jonathan said calmly, "I hugged my lucky walnut and jammed the throttle to the floor. *Pedal to the metal*, as you Yanks say." And he *was* gaining, his front fender was actually out in front as the gray rock wall which made up the side of the tunnel roared up directly in front of him! Would he have room? Would he have time?

Jonathan sighed and stuck a roadside timothy weed in his teeth. For a long moment he watched the puffy clouds float by overhead. "I woke in St. Vincent's with my arms and legs stuck out like a scarecrow," he said. "I was frozen in a plaster body cast with tubes running in and out, like you see sometimes in one of those funny joke get well cards."

"Some lucky walnut," Niki scoffed.

Jonathan stood and stretched, yawning in the warm October sunlight. He looked like he was getting immense joy out of the day. I could see the scar on the side of his neck that ran down into his fireproof racing uniform, and knew there had to be more tracks and stitches all over his body.

"Hey," he said gently to Nikita, "I'm still alive."

He reached in the flap of his jacket pocket and pulled out a small, round object so we both could see it. After seeming to study it for a moment, he winked and tossed it to me. Then he walked away, whistling "Ma Michelle" as he headed toward his low-slung Ferrari, which waited by the curving white road guard at the end of the straight.

I kept that lucky walnut for years, in an old jacket of mine. In fact, I'm sure I still have it somewhere, hanging in the back of an old closet. It's comforting to know it's there, because today the world is too often a harried, troubling and even hopeless place. And in times like these it's good to have a little something that reaffirms your belief in the luck of the moment.

Facing Bullitt

People who know about such things will tell you there are only two kinds of actors: method actors like Meryl Streep and Dustin Hoffman who can play anybody, and presence players like John Wayne and maybe Tom Cruise who can only play themselves. This is interesting, as far as broad and general theories go, but in the life of a real star things can get a little more complicated. Take somebody like Steve McQueen, surely one of those presence players with his haunting, lonely stare and minimalist facial gestures.

I worked with Steve in the early 1970's, and the rumor back then--a rumor that doesn't seem to go away--was that Steve in real life had taken on the persona of many of his earlier movie characters.

After he played the cool international mastermind in <u>The Thomas Crown Affair</u>, the story goes, he was never able to snap completely back out of that role in his real life and *be himself* again. Of course, that assumes any of us knows completely who we are, and if you look around you, you'll see self-ignorance abounds. Still, when Steve got in big money trouble on <u>Bullitt</u>, his classic police detective thriller, he played high stakes financial poker with the studios the way Thomas Crown would have. As the costs soared and the studio threatened to rein him in and shut down the production, he put up his entire stake to personally invest in the picture, gambling every cent he owned on its ultimate success. And when <u>Bullitt</u> played really big at the box office, Steve/Thomas Crown personally raked in millions. Suddenly he had the money to go along with the persona.

It wasn't just about money. The legends say that Steve himself raced Bullitt's hot Ford Mustang over San Francisco's hilly streets, just as he was supposed to have jumped his own bike for the key sequence in <u>The Great Escape</u>. Steve would never deny it (and nobody dared ask to his face), even though those exploits well may have been created by eager and inventive public relations flacks. (I can call them that, having been one myself, and knowing how they/we think.) It is true that people who were on the set for those pictures later told their friends that Buddy Ekins jumped the bike in the one picture and George Robotham handled the hot Mustang in the other. Regardless, Steve once again began to live his own legend as he took to racing cars and bikes in earnest.

So, was there any truth to the rumor that the man was living his movie roles in real life? You decide. By 1968, he had the image of a wealthy, exciting, dangerous and mysterious international loner with a passion for rolling the dice of life and racing fast cars. (He may not have picked up the added overtone of loving incredibly gorgeous women until Ali MacGraw and <u>The Getaway</u>.)

It's hard to say exactly when he caught the auteur filmmaker bug that infected so many of us in *The Love Generation*. He may have had it all along, that particular disease sometimes taking a while to become virulent. I do know that by the time he started working on the set of <u>Le Mans</u>, where Nikita Knatz and I were set to shoot the featurette, <u>Le Mans & the Man McQueen</u>, the signs were everywhere. Steve's arms would weave and wave and

words like *happening* and *creatively expressive* and
capturing the moment would come out of his mouth and
everything would be a grand mush upon the ears of
anyone listening without the cushion of true fan bliss.

Niki and I were to create the story of the making of
that particular racing movie, and we did so in a short film
that is still considered a classic of the genre. But here's
a bit of the real story, a few short strokes from the tale
we were never allowed to tell:

As he came to France to begin his racing movie,
Steve was much affected by the enormously successful
Woodstock Festival documentary. He wanted his racing
movie to capture the same sort of rough-and-ready,
shoot-around-the-clock 16-millimeter *cinema verite.*
That meant, among other things, that he didn't want to
act a role, *per se.* He didn't want to read what he
considered to be phony lines or have a story involved
with what he thought were foolish plots. He wanted no
heavy human drama getting in the way of what he saw
as the ultimate drama of his picture--drivers facing death
for glory in the race itself.

So, in Steve's mind, this was going to be a pure
racing documentary movie, the most realistic movie ever
made about racing, which Steve had begun to refer to as
a blood sport. Unfortunately, that's not the script he sold
to CBS Cinema Center, the studio to whom he'd sold the
project and the people who were funding his dream.
That picture, the initial script he sold the studios, was
your standard dramatic fare, an exciting grand prix
racing picture with just the right dollops of romance,
violence and death mixed in. You can see how
diametrically opposed that proposal was from the project
he set out to create.

Who was going to be in creative control? Well,
that's a complex and difficult question. The studio, of
course, thought they had control. And they delegated
that control to famous director John Sturges, the man
who had given Steve his first big break in <u>The Great</u>

<u>Escape</u>. With Sturges at the helm, the North Hollywood-based studio could be confident their money and trust was on solid ground and the project would proceed steadily to its successful and profitable conclusion. In reality, nothing would be further from the truth.

Showing up in France at the fabled Le Mans race track, 2nd Unit Director Jack Reddish began shooting running racing car footage, the sleek autos flashing through the rural countryside before racing through the stands area and back out into the countryside for more loops. This was dangerous and expensive stuff, and pretty enough on screen, but after some months they had yet to shoot a single frame with Steve in it. And worse, Steve was telling John Sturges more and more exactly how he wanted *his racing film* shot. After the 2nd unit had shot 120,000 feet of gorgeous racing footage, and he had shot nearly nothing, Sturges stormed back to the U.S., claiming it was "the worst experience of his professional life". And the movie went on what the trade magazines politely call *extended hiatus.* That little vacation went on for eight weeks. Steve went back to North Hollywood to explain it all. He must have been very persuasive, because the moneymen didn't shut the thing down then and there.

Production was resumed with three competing writers, including the famous script doctor John T. Kelley and Playboy racing writer Ken Purdy, all three working in adjoining trailers on different versions of what they hoped would be shot the next day--and none of it was much like the original script Steve's Solar Productions had originally pitched and sold. John Sturges was replaced by the polished and dapper Lee Katzin, who immediately found himself with the tiger by the tail. Nothing seemed to please Steve, who had taken up residence in a classic French countryside villa and then torn up the 200-year-old gardens and turned them into a motocross where he and his friends could jump their bikes.

The mood on the set thickened and turned ugly. If Steve didn't like the new pages at all, he wouldn't come out of his big motor home, which was parked near the track. He would send out word he was sick. One day, as if to prove his illness, he staggered out looking grey as a slab of limestone. The crew, most of whom had read Forsyth's The Day of the Jackal, accused him of chewing cordite to change his complexion. Incredible as it sounds, Steve once roared out of his cabana and towed Lee across the set with a firm grasp on his trademark necktie, yelling for the entire assembled cast and crew to hear that he, Steve McQueen, would kiss Lee's ass in a window of Macy's department store in Manhattan if the footage of him would be turning out right, but it *just-wasn't-turning-out-RIGHT!* Much to Lee's credit (or discredit, depending on how you think about such matters) he hung in there. Without his tenacity, Le Mans would never have been completed. But none of it came easy.

Viewing it today, you have to be struck by the feeling that Le Mans comes about as close to *cinema verite* as can be achieved using huge and bulky 70 millimeter cameras and surly French union camera crews that couldn't seem to get a first shot off until 11 o'clock in the morning. But, if you were there experiencing it, the general run of it was grief and agony all around, dissatisfaction and ill will in the air and an overall feeling of gloom.

I'd had a little trouble with McQueen, myself. In spite of Niki's warning (Nikita knew Steve much better than I) I'd wanted to ride along in the tiny passenger seat and film the great man while he was driving. Steve had treated my request like it was impossible, and I must have indicated with a graceless sneer or some other mannerism that it didn't take a superhuman to climb in a race car. That was my attitude problem; I'd been called on it before, and it didn't endear me to our star.

A month went by before I saw him again. I was back in the States, working at our offices on Radford near Cinema Center. Late one night, I was hunched over a moviola to stick the footage together when Steve unexpectedly walked in. He sat on a stool looking over my shoulder while I ran the trailer for him, and then his hands started going and he described thousands of dollars worth of new footage and expensive optical dissolves he wanted to add to our little epic.

"An eagle," he said, "I see this beautiful slow-motion eagle, wings spread, back-lit by the sun. We cross-dissolve to a shot of me looking into the distance, and then to a shot of the Porsche. You see, we have to somehow *symbolize,* through the use of *symbols,* the tremendous feeling of *freedom,* of *exhilaration,* of *pure, raw energy,* that one has when behind the wheel of a racing machine."

"Great ideas, Steve," I said. "But we can't do that."

He stood, and the musing look fled from his face. The creative filmmaker had vanished. I was left alone with Thomas Crown. With the dangerous Bullitt. He stared at me. The room grew dark and smoky. All I could see were those famous eyes of his, those flinty, relentless eyes. *I'm in a fricking movie,* I remember thinking. *Steve has put me in a gunfight...only I'm the bad guy.*

I feel embarrassed today that I could be put under his spell so easily, or that I could have acted so foolishly, but that presence of his was so powerful, it just sucked me in. I stood and faced him, knocking over the editor's stool and terribly conscious of my hands at my sides. *As the bad guy, wasn't I supposed to draw first?*

My voice actually got hoarse, probably from fright.

"Steve," I said. "I can't. We can't."

"Why not, Jack?" he asked in a voice that was like a whispery knife-edge.

"Steve, we don't have the money. And Cinema Center isn't going to pony up."

"Oh," he said.

And his mood lightened, shifting us both out of the scene as if a hypnotist in some other dimension had snapped his fingers. No reason for a shoot-out; I wasn't contradicting his *filmic creativity.* It was just about money.

"You should have said so in the first place," he said, coming over and clapping me on the back. "I'll get those bastards to cough up."

Maybe he tried and maybe he didn't. I never heard any more about it. And when Niki and I gathered everybody who mattered together in a screening room at the studio and ran the final answer print, Steve McQueen loved it. At least, whoever showed up that day in his whipcord lean body and behind that enigmatic little smile on his face said that he did.

The Legend of Jake Barstow

Back when Nikita Knatz and I did the classic[1] featurette for Steve McQueen's racing picture <u>Le Mans</u>, we divided up the credits fair and square; he took "Director" and I took "Writer/Producer". But the truth is, Niki and I actually did *everything*, from the first glimmer of an idea to the last frame of finished film, in the true tradition of the lost underground filmmakers of the 60's. Niki sold the idea to Steve and to the money boys, and he art directed and drew some pictures for the titles. He and I both worked as cameramen/directors, lighting guys and soundmen. When the time came to post, I cut the film, mixed the sound and conformed the footage into A & B rolls.

Of course, this being Hollywood, we didn't want to seem small-time, so whenever there was something to be delivered to the lab, reels to be picked up or any other menial task, we got Jake Barstow to do it. Jake was an incredible guy. He loaded cameras. He cut film. He made coffee. He ran errands. He did a hundred other things. And, as we had made him up out of thin air, we didn't have to pay him a dime. Good thing. With

[1] In America, where such things are largely ignored, people remember the featurette, but not who made it. In the European film community, Nikita and I are as minor deities.

what Cinema Center was giving us to do the film, we couldn't have afforded anything more.

By contrast, the official and approved Hollywood way to create things is quite set in concrete; filmmaking is a team sport. Important decisions are made after great howls and much committee beating of the brush. By custom, whichever mid-level executive is able to bang his chest the loudest frightens away the others and gets his way. Before, between and after these rituals, actual work is done by common workers who are labeled according to function, and there are hundreds of functions. In general, writers do not presume to direct, set designers don't presume to talk costumes, and cameramen are terribly polite to lighting men. In general, I said.

Niki and I ran into some of this in France. The day after I got there, a Belgian cameraman refused to do a shot for us because he said it was too dangerous. Just walked off the set. The silly fool, unaccustomed to *sub rosa* filmmaking, naturally assumed that was going to shut our operation down until we ran after him and forked across a bushel basket full of Francs. *Not going to happen, Pierre.* I got behind the right rear tire of a remote-controlled Ferrari and pointed the 12-120 Angenieux zoom lens on my 16 mm camera at the dark rubber. Niki leaned over the guardrail and held me by the back of my belt and the scruff of my neck. He was built like a weight lifter; in spite of dire warnings all around, I was sure he could jerk me clean off the track if the car decided to spin out of control and run over our camera position (as it had done the day before).

The engine gave a few thunderous revs and the red car bolted away from us, accelerating down the track. At the right moment, the remote-control driver twitched his little controls and the speeding Ferrari hit the guardrail, launching itself 30 feet in the air to smash in spectacular fashion through a big wooden Martini-Rossi sign. And Niki and I had captured it all on film. We actually had the best master shot of anybody, remote-control crashing not being an exact science and several of the huge locked-down Panavision cameras missing the action entirely. Producer Bob Rosen told us later that if we'd been using 35 mm, he'd have used our shot in the movie itself.

Anyway, after we got back to the States, one day Niki and I were sitting around our office in Studio City (there really is such a place) waiting for fame and fortune to drop by when some geek from the cameraman's union came sniffing around, asking about who had done the work on our featurette. This guy was wearing shiny pants three sizes too small for his stomach, which flopped over to help hide the fact he'd forgotten his belt. There were wet circles on his shirt under his armpits, and a quick look over at my partner assured me Niki wasn't impressed either.

"Why?" I asked. "You want to hire us?"

The guy didn't think that was funny. "I've seen your little film," he said through pursed lips. "You've combined footage that somebody from your unit shot with footage that was obviously shot by union cameramen working on the movie."

"So what?" Niki said, throwing his foot over the remaining empty chair in the room.

"So that means you got a mixed crew, union and non-union, and *that* means whoever shot that footage is in deep shit."

Niki's eyebrows came down. He could clean out a surly barroom when he was of a mind to, and it didn't take much to put him in the mood. "Yeah?" he said. "What could happen to him? You gonna take away his camera? Or maybe roll a crab dolly over him?"

The geek's frown deepened and he took a rumpled notepad from his back pocket, one of those little ones with the wire spiral that always seems to be unwinding.

"What are you doing?" I asked.

"Just give me the name," he said wearily. "I want the name of your cameraman."

"And if we choose not to rat on him?"

The guy really got pissy. "You don't understand," he said. "We could put you out of business." He poked his pencil at me for emphasis, "Now I don't want to have to do that. Just give me the name."

I shrugged and shook my head. Niki was grinning at me. He quickly frowned as the union guy turned toward him.

"A *Camera*man...", Niki said, as if he couldn't get over the wonder of it. "I never thought that dirty bastard would get us in so much trouble."

I leaned back and looked at my hiking boots, which were all scuffed and battered. "You're not going to *tell who it is?!*"

"I guess we got no choice, partner." He sighed and gave the guy his mean look, "Okay, mister, you win. But I don't want you coming back around here bothering us no more. You come back here, I don't know, I might break your leg."

"The name of the cameraman."

"His name is Jake Barstow. Dirty, rotten, no-good Barstow, bringing all this trouble to us." Niki tossed him a typed list, "See. It's right there on the credits."

"We'll catch him and send him packing," the geek said with a grim little smile. He carefully printed the name on his notepad and slipped it back in his pocket.

"Good," Niki said. "And when you do, tell him who it was that snitched on him."

How to Get Your Director's Card

Back in the day, the problem I faced trying to join the prestigious Directors Guild of America was the same one any enterprising young man has trying to get into any shop that tries to protect its members. The applicant needs to have a card to get work, but you have to have worked to get your card. Sure, the DGA, the WGA and the other Hollywood unions and guilds have programs to help you get in, but the process is anything but swift and it drives a lot of bright young kids who don't have the staying power right back to Iowa and Indiana...where, ironically, the chances are often better that you can get your card.

When I first moved to Hollywood in the late 1960's, old-time director Arthur Pierson tried to persuade me to join the DGA. But at the time I was writing and directing low-budget documentaries, educationals and marketing films for Hanna-Barbera, and the last thing HB wanted was to pay me guild wages--and be forced to hire an assistant director on top of that. So becoming a *bona fide* guild director was one of those impossible dreams. I didn't know any guild signatory company who was willing to take a chance on me, and so as the Dawn of Aquarius pushed boldly into the 1970's, I was driven nearly to financial ruin by the effort and outlay it took to make the Le Mans featurette. My wife and I packed our bags and retreated to Detroit where I'd accepted a writer/producer job with Grey Advertising, working on the Ford Corporate account. Once in the Motor City, I was amazed at the amount of money clients were paying for the same services I'd been practically giving away in Hollywood. Nikita and I had completed the Le Mans featurette for $30,000. In Detroit that wouldn't even buy a 30-second radio spot.

Not that they liked paying big money for their television and radio commercials. In fact, when I got there, our clients were screaming over the cost of production. Ford Motor Company executives prided themselves on being hard-nosed, no-nonsense mavericks, and at this time Ford's head of advertising and marketing was a real tough nut, the legendary John J. Morrissey, known simply as "JJ". If anybody hated spending money on film production, JJ was the man.

Now if you're used to book publishing or film production, you know a novel or a movie can take years from concept until it shows up on the bookshelves or in the theaters. Things aren't like that in the ad biz. A marketing exec's bad dream, research guru's badly pointing chart or a bad blip in sales and a new campaign will be in the works overnight. I came to Detroit with a big head of steam--I was the guy responsible for that *terrific Steve McQueen racing documentary.* The guy who'd hired me left and I swiftly rose to Head of Broadcast Production.

For the first pool of commercials we did after I took over, I hired local Detroit producer Dick Gagnon (agency producers and even agency heads of production don't actually produce anything--they just hire outside producers and outside commercial production companies). Gagnon recommended hot New York commercial director Peter Miranda at $7 grand a day. Imagine, $7,000 a day in 1972! Still, that was about average for a so-called hot director. We went to San Francisco, though we could have shot anywhere, and we hired producer/director Greg Snazelle to provide the cameras, crew, locationing and so on, what's known as *the basic below-the-line package.*

Now if the cost of those spots wasn't enough to put me already in hot water, the director of choice was sure to get me there; Peter Miranda didn't get to be a name in the business by simply shooting the commercials as they were written, storyboarded and approved by the client. Actually, very few successful commercial directors do that. The only way they can become advertising legends is by providing *added value,* and the way they do that is by coming up with special filmic looks and their own personal interpretations that somehow make the commercials *better.*

Peter Miranda was a classic commercial director, a man much influenced by the likes of John Ford, and his framings were generally magnificent. But to get *the Miranda Look,* he tended to stray further and further from the boards. For instance, our Ford Corporate "Stranded Car" spot was supposed to be shot on a two-lane blacktop. The poor, stranded family with their broken car was supposed to wait out the day while heartless cars whizzed past. The underlying idea (what the *cogni scenti* in that world of chromium leopards and little czars call *the basic concept*) was that with Ford warranty service this wouldn't happen to you. The concept aside, Peter loved the light that came from the Pacific, so for his two-lane blacktop, he directed us to a military reservation north of the Golden Gate Bridge where he selected an unpaved trail that ran along the very rim of a vertical cliff 600 feet over the ocean waves crashing straight below on a rocky shore. Dangerous. And, the only passing traffic we got all day was a motorbike rider who, not expecting a big Ford motorcar sitting in his bike trail, nearly plummeted to his death on the rocky beach below.

Peter's idea was to lock down the camera and cross-dissolve to the same shot, so the only things which would change would be the position of the family and the lighting, which, as we were shooting in a western direction, would slowly go from front-lit to top-lit to rim-lit to back-lit and finally to a darkening silhouette. This was something the art director hadn't thought of in his wildest dreams, and I tried to have Miranda's approach killed, but the Grey Creative Director, who agreed with Miranda that the original boards were dull and boring, was now doing ecstatic handstands. Peter also insisted that our suave corporate spokesman, Leslie Nielsen, couldn't possibly appear in this commercial, as he would spoil the isolated feeling of the commercial which the CD, the writer and the art director now saw as an award winner they could stick on their escape reels. However, Peter assured me we would be using Leslie for the voice-over narration, and this would appease the client.

Peter also came up with ideas to "fix" the other spots as well, but they weren't such drastic or expensive departures. The prep days passed and we shot Miranda's three little epics, and then Peter treated the agency to dinner at L'Etoile, a 5-star French restaurant, and Gagnon and Snazelle hosted us for a Sunday afternoon outing on Greg's antique classic 40-foot teakwood cruiser, puttering around San Francisco Bay while some of the world's most gorgeous women made empty conversation and filled our wine glasses. It was easy to see why commercial production cost so much.

The original signed budget had been for $90,000, actually a small sum for a project of that sort in that corner of the world at that time. However, the stranded car commercial involved lots of overages. Peter had wanted a "flat" long-lens look, and so decided to shoot with a 1,200 mm lens from across a ravine. Since film registration would be critical or the dissolves wouldn't match perfectly, we had to rent the finest and most expensive Panavision equipment. The camera had to remain absolutely motionless for a 12-hour period. Unfortunately, even though we heavily sandbagged the tripod, over that period the heavy long lens sagged the camera down a minute fraction in the hours between each shot. This meant we had to re-register all the footage in the labs, a costly process. Also, no one had considered what would happen when the evening fog came in, all pearly and beautiful and making the lighting almost impossible to calculate. We had to find the right settings only later on in the lab, using a Hazeltine projector to find the narrowest of bands where the film would still print the images with the necessary clarity. These and other factors more than doubled the bill.

I'll never forget the look on John J. Morrissey's face as he saw the stranded car commercial for the first time. He kept looking back and forth from the storyboards to what he was seeing on the screen. This was a very, very bad sign, as there wasn't anything similar there. His mouth was open. His eyes flickered madly when the commercial got to the place where Leslie Nielsen was supposed to appear and didn't. I could practically hear his inner voice screaming, *We're paying that Hollywood hotshot six figures a year to do VOICE-OVERS?!*

JJ turned to us, grasping for words. There was a long silence as his face turned from red to purple.

Finally, all he could think to say was, "Who the hell was that geek on the motorbike?"

Nobody knew what exactly to say to that, and it was about then that JJ found his voice. It all came out in one of the bloodiest client meetings I've ever attended. Morrissey was magnificent in his outrage. He roared on and on about *the artsy-fartsy look* of the lighting and raged about the costly financial overages. Our account guys tried to counterattack, but it was hopeless, particularly after one of them let the princely sum of Miranda's day rate slip out in the open...three days and three prep days. With that JJ went over the top, berserk as a hyena on LSD. And like I knew it would, the frothing madness turned in my direction. The client became deadly quiet and everybody in the room knew my head was about to roll. No question about it, you could bet the farm, the *Hot Shit from Hollywood* (advertising people are often not kind) was about to crash and burn.

"You're supposed to be our resident genius from Tinseltown", Morrissey said calmly. "I thought *you* were a director. Do *you* charge $7,000 a day?"

"No, I don't," I said. I was angry with myself that I hadn't stood up to Miranda a bit more, and cringing at the thought of the cold steel that was about to hit my neck.

"Fine," JJ said. "Then *you* direct the commercials from now on."

It took me a beat or two to catch up.

"Ahh, I don't think the guys in this room are going to go for that..." I muttered.

"WHAT guys?!" Morrissey roared. Nobody moved a muscle, nobody said a word.

And with that, I saw a clear path for myself.

"I'm sorry," I said, "but I'm not in the Directors Guild--and I don't intend to become a scab."

It was the perfect thing to say, Detroit being the union town it was.

"Then you *join the Directors Guild,*" he ordered. His eyes swept the room. "Any problems with that?"

"No problems," I said.

"No problems, JJ," they all repeated.

In the next few days, the agency fired the Creative Director, who violently disagreed with our new direction, and we spent the rest of the month developing a simple newscaster format for Leslie Nielsen to pitch the outrageous claim that Ford Service Bays were pleasant and joyful places from which emanated NO UNHAPPY OWNERS. I created a subsidiary corporation for Grey, a wholly owned outside production company called

Creative Dimensions, and we subcontracted with video houses in L.A. for stage, crew and equipment.

Arthur Pierson sponsored me at the Directors Guild of America, and I could get in easily now that I showed a steady stream of upcoming work (with a guild-signatory company that insisted I direct), and the advertising agency even paid my entrance fee into the guild. In the following two years, I directed over 250 Ford Corporate commercials before JJ got bored and decided to try something else. By that time I had my card and the experience, and was ready for something new. Lynnie and I and our family packed our things and headed back west to California where I used my union wages for a down deposit on a modest hillside house in Woodland Hills.

So if you find your direct path to show biz greatness is blocked by red tape, paperwork, bad luck or lack of opportunity, sometimes a strategic retreat to the distant provinces of filmmaking can get you the things you need to get ahead. At least, that's the way it worked for me.

Naughty Natalie

Back in the 50's my dad and two other guys owned their own steel-busting company in South Chicago Heights. It was called Industrial Welding, and by the time they paid the bills there was barely enough money left to pass around. So during the interminably endless period when I was a gawky teenager I didn't get to the movies much. But when I did go, they affected me in ways that probably linger even today. For some odd reason, I still have an affection for wearing my collar up, and I like to lean against walls like an old walrus with an attitude, waiting for something to happen.

Well, years went by. I actually became a filmmaker and, one day, something did happen. The phone rang and it was producer Harold Orton and his sidekick Hal Hamilton calling from Jolly Old England. They were coming to L.A. to shoot a set of exquisite Lux Beauty Soap commercials, and would I be the American producer? The spots were to be directed by then up-and-coming Brit director Peter Yates, and shot by stellar cameraman Jacques Coquillion. And they were starring Natalie Wood.

You know the cameraman is the big secret of any shoot, no matter what anybody tells you. He's the one who can take average material and give you that just-right look that puts it over the top, and cameramen never get enough credit for what they do. On the other hand, it didn't hurt to have Natalie, either. This was in the mid-seventies, and she was absolutely gorgeous, a woman in full flower, as they say.

Being a producer is nothing like what you might imagine. Aside from brief moments when one gets to display big shot cunning and guile, the rest of the time passes taking phone calls from the aloof, the desperate and the greedy, setting up locations and catering, haggling with cast and crew and finally just sitting around waiting for things to happen, assuming the director even lets you on the set. Working as American producer for Harold and Hal, I got to do all those things except the cunning and guile part.

The commercials, for which Natalie was being paid $40,000, a princely sum at that time, have never been shown in the U.S. It was a part of the contract, the top stars not wanting their adoring American public to know they stooped to sell common artifacts of human consumption like soap and beer. Anyway, the idea behind these spots was to show a day in the glamorous life of a Hollywood star. We were shooting Natalie on the set, Natalie at her magnificent home in Palos Verdes, Natalie riding a horse through the flowered meadows of Bell Canyon, Natalie applying the rich creamy lather of Lux Beauty Soap to her face and rinsing it to show how pure and smooth it left her skin, and finally Natalie at dusk getting out of an antique limo at the posh Beverly Wilshire Hotel, ready for a fabulous night on the town.

Of course, it wasn't Natalie's real home, horse, limo or soap, but that never really matters in commercials, which are hardly carved from the elemental stuff of life. Peter Yates had gotten his start in the biz shooting TV spots, so he knew what was expected of him. His directing was quick, gentle and clever, Jacques made Natalie look as lovely on film as she really was, the catering was a cut above the ordinary, and the day moved along with no problems. *Hey, hey, hey, as Yogi Bear might say, When's the last time this happened?*

Things kept falling into place, shot after shot ticking off without a problem. Even the all-important beauty shots of Natalie with the soap bar went off without a hitch. We got the last of her loveliness in the can an hour early.

Yates had called the wrap and we were breaking up from the Beverly Wilshire to go our separate ways when Harold asked if I would drive our star to her home, located just a few miles away on Canon Drive in Beverly Hills. I said I would, and in another minute Natalie, her hairdresser/makeup person, and her costumer piled into the back of my Volkswagen van and we pulled away from the hotel.

We hadn't gone two blocks when the subject turned to silk panties. Natalie's costumer had found a special ladies shop where the two ladies had bought some scanty fine things, and this turned into a discussion of how silk felt against flesh, the see-through qualities of the various fabrics, and unique designs that served a variety of functions other than sleep. The hairdresser/makeup person who was sort of a man, kept chiming in with his own experience in these matters, and I alone didn't have anything to add to the conversation. I felt like exactly who I was, a rough bumbler from South Chicago who had somehow managed to connive his way into the outer fringes of the incredible and glorious movie business.

I sat alone up front and kept my eyes on the road as the van rolled along past the famous boutiques and salons of Beverly Hills. When we got to her place, which was just a few houses north of Santa Monica Boulevard, I turned into the driveway and pulled to a stop. Natalie gave me a wicked look and said, "My, my, driver, but you haven't said a word. Cat got your tongue?"

The hairdresser/makeup person snickered, "Maybe our subject matter is a little too *advanced* for him."

She grinned at me, "Is that right, *driver*?"

Natalie knew I was the American producer of our little shoot, but she'd been a studio brat all her life, and she knew how to push all the buttons. It worked, all right. I could feel that old sullen, heavy-blooded feeling starting to take over. I knew my collar was up, the way it always was. *Once in a lifetime,* I thought. *This was a one-in-a-million chance, and it was happening to me.* I threw my arm over the seat back, idly, like I didn't have a care in the world, and leaned toward her. Stealing from at least two James Dean movies, I drawled in what I desperately hoped was a decent imitation of that humble-sincere-yet-joking way he had, "We sure are a long way from Rebel Without A Cause, ain't we, missy?"

Maybe she had left a roast in the oven or had to get going so she could try on her latest pair of laced under things. She didn't say. But I knew there would be no more joking at my expense. A look came over her face like she'd been reminded of something long-ago that had been important to her. She studied me for a moment and then gave me a little nod. It wasn't a happy or a friendly gesture, but I knew she understood and respected what I had done. And then she pulled back the sliding door and was gone.

She came a long way, Natalie did, and she spent most of her life on the set, hanging around glittery movie people as she worked her way to the top of the biz. But we all go a long way in our lives, no matter who we are or what we do. Years later, when I read in The Reporter that it had ended badly for her, I thought back to that time when I drove her home in my van. And I remembered how once, for a few seconds, two people-- the great star and one of her millions of fans--saw things eye-to-eye and for a brief moment understood a little bit about each other.

The Jackie Shoot

On the set, the director is king, master and high overlord. Anybody who saw Peter O'Toole in <u>The Stunt Man</u>, the best movie ever made about filmmaking, knows that. But few realize that the power behind the director is always the 1st Assistant Director. It is actually harder to become an assistant director than it is to become a director, which is why there are far less assistants than directors.

To direct, all you have to do is bamboozle your way into the job, write a script that everybody has to have, for instance, and tie yourself to it as director. But to *assistant* direct, you have to know what you are doing. Many productions imperiled by young, weak, untalented, bumbling or crazed directors have been saved by grizzled old assistants.

Which is why, when Harold Orton returned once again from England, this time to capture the rare and particular loveliness that is Jacqueline Bisset in his commercials for Lux Beauty Soap, I should have been more concerned than I was. For Harold, cutting corners, planned to go it *sans* an assistant director.

On previous visits he had used able Hal Hamilton to assist director Peter Yates. But now, Peter was busy prepping his new movie <u>Breaking Away</u>, and we were to make do with Bryan Forbes, somewhat of an *enfant terrible*. Still, he had the right credits for Lux; he was *big time,* known for helming such pictures as The L-Shaped Room, King Rat, and The Stepford Wives.

Bryan, I was told, was not much accustomed to the hit-and-run and make-do brand of improvisation that makes for a good commercial shoot. All the more reason to bring on a Hal Hamilton. Even with Yates, who had cut his teeth on commercials, I'd felt Hal, who has since made a name for himself writing, producing and directing an impressive body of work in Europe, was an essential member of the crew. But, if Harold was concerned, he didn't show it.

"Not to worry, Jack," he said. "I doubt Bryan will need much help. And, if he does, I'll fill in, myself. Between the two of us, you and I can surely cover it."

"I don't think I'll be much help," I warned. In my role as American Producer, I operated much as a Unit Production Manager. I was responsible for cast, crew, locations, lighting, catering, permits--all the detail work. There was no time in my day to hang over the director's shoulder.

Harold's response was predictably Ortonian, "Not to worry, Jack."

Unlike the fantasy lives of other great stars that Harold and I had filmed for Lux--Natalie Wood in Hollywood and Ali MacGraw in New York City--the "Jackie Shoot", as Harold called it, would have at least one element of truth. She lived in a wonderful stone-and-glass house with a Chinese garden lush with bamboo and a small brook that bubbled over round stones. We would be able to capture the "at home" and the critical "beauty lather" shots here, and so wouldn't have to find (and pay for) other locations.

Harold was ecstatic.

"See, Jack?" he said, the sly and cunning grin spreading over his wrinkled old face, "Everything as planned."

But none of us had planned on Bryan Forbes. Our problems began just before lunch, when Harold was harassed by a series of trans-Atlantic calls to iron out final copy. He asked me to cover Forbes, but I was in the middle of lining up the next day's shoot, which was to be in San Francisco.

"Well, then", Harold shrugged, "Our director will just have to muckle through for a few moments without us, won't he?"

But nobody'd measured Bryan's capacity to muckle. I returned from the phones to find him pouting and looking off into the distant tops of some palm trees. The crew was sitting around, waiting for his next move, and our star was nowhere to be seen. Harold returned to gape over my shoulder. Having worked with him before, I could read his mind: *This was, indeed, costly inactivity*.

"Who is my assistant?" Forbes demanded.

"He is!" Harold and I both said in the same moment, each pointing a finger at the other.

"So. I have two assistants, and no assistance!"

Harold looked around as if perhaps the problem would pop up and identify itself. Nothing did. "What is the specific matter which holds us up at this moment?" he asked in his brisk *let's fix this and get the camera rolling* producer voice.

"Our Jackie was beginning to perspire. The makeup artist--whom I have been informed also doubles as hairdresser" (here he shot Harold an accusing look), "was out of tissues. Doing both jobs, you'd think she'd have double tissues, wouldn't you? But no. Not one bloody tissue on this set, and neither of you two assistants in sight."

Harold couldn't believe it. He was still looking around as if expecting Jacqueline to return with a batch of lilies on her arm, saying it was all a joke.

"So you took a break?" There were a hundred other things your average commercial director would have done in Bryan's stead. Harold, who was admittedly a little extreme, would have used the shirt off his back, a towel from the kitchen or the rag the cameraman uses to wipe his lens, before he'd have allowed the shoot to grind to a halt over a little sweat.

"I will not proceed under these conditions."

"Jack will get you your tissues." I could see Harold grinding his teeth as he walked away.

I ran and fetched a dusty box of Kleenex from my van. As I handed them to the makeup person, Bryan started blathering at me not to leave his side, ever again, until he had completed the very last shot of this production.

"I'm sorry, Mr. Forbes," I said. "I've got to go pay the catering truck, or he'll take the food back. You'd better talk to Harold."

But Harold was on the phone again, clearly upset over which adjectives were the absolutely right ones to express the miracle which takes place when the creamy lather of Lux comes in contact with a woman's face. I had my foot on the front bumper of the catering truck and was signing a check for a burly, skeptical driver when I heard a sort of blubbery, whimpering roar with an English accent going on in the middle distance.

It was our director reading Harold his final rights. I returned just as Harold was permanently assigning me to Forbes. Harold would take over my duties. I was not to leave Bryan's side for any reason, and was to heed his every beck and call.

"Why not?" I shrugged.

I could see Forbes' lip curl. Obviously, I should have genuflected.

"All right, Mr. Forbes. Shall we begin?" I said. I couldn't bring myself to say "sir"; the words not being able to form themselves in my mouth. It seemed at that unlucky moment I was having one of my recurring attacks of recalcitrance. It's something genetic, I'm told, and very, very bad for my career.

But our director only looked at his watch, "Perhaps we'd better break for lunch..."

I thought Harold, who had returned to see what this new delay was all about, would give birth to a giraffe or something. His face got red and he started to puff up like a tropical fish. *Professional* directors didn't break for lunch when they were behind. They made up the shots, and then they ate. And if they couldn't make them up, they shot with a sandwich in their hand and mumbled "Action!" with their mouths stuffed with linguini. But Forbes was already miffed, so Harold gave in and started to wander over to the catering truck.

Then Bryan dropped his second bombshell and the shouting started all over again. It seems he wanted to run over to the Fox lot for a meeting, which may well have been the reason why he'd started the fuss over the facial tissues in the first place. He promised to be back within the hour, but Harold yelped and refused to give in, seeing his afternoon half-gone before his director returned.

That's when both men turned to me. Bryan, now believing he owned me body and soul as is the eternal pact between directors and their First Assistants, said, "You. You're the Hollywood expert. I say, twenty minutes each way. Fifteen minutes for my meeting. That makes fifty-five minutes. Tell our friend Harold here that I will make it with time to spare."

"You don't have a prayer, pal."

"What?!" His word was like a rifle shot. If I was to be forgiven, it wasn't going to be in this life. "You don't know what you're talking about, you...you worthless person!"

"Maybe not, Bryan. But you won't be back in an hour. In fact, if you're back here inside of an hour and a half, I'll give you $50 of my own money!"

Bryan looked around at the American members of the crew for support, but they were all busy punching the stopwatch buttons on their watches. He stamped his foot like The Little Prince, and stormed away to his car.

We sat around for two hours, eating lukewarm lasagna and drinking lightly cooled cokes, waiting for the return of the prodigal director. I could see by the look in Harold's eyes that in another few minutes our cameraman was going to be promoted to cameraman/director.

But Forbes showed up just shy of the event horizon, muttering about "extraordinary

Harold & the Coke Sniffers

I guess I do know the meaning of intrepid. When I think of that word, I will forever conjure up the image of a slight, grey-haired Englishman standing firm against three angry New York goons who want to pound him into the ground. The man is Harold Orton. And the three ugly fisters want to take a chunk of his money away from him. I'll tell you what a man can do against odds like that.

When this happened, in the late 1970's, nobody really knew how old Harold was. The common guess was *very* old, but I know for a fact that he lived nearly to the end of the millennium. One of the very best English film producers that few average filmgoers ever heard of, Harold had been around practically since Tommy Edison invented the machine, and he'd filmed everywhere in the world from the pyramids of Egypt to the Babylonian walks of Hollywood. Harold was known for three things: his strict professionalism, his unflagging civility under pressure, and his legendary flinty ways with a buck.

It was the summer of 1978. I'd worked on two other projects with him; the first with Natalie Wood, and the second with Jacqueline Bisset (when His Cheapness had gotten me in trouble with director Bryan Forbes). Now Harold was flying in from London to do the next pool in his series of exquisite Lux Beauty Soap commercials, this time starring Ali MacGraw. We would photograph Ali at an 18th Century country estate in New Jersey, living the country life. Then we would show her shopping at Bloomingdale's, perhaps graciously signing the autograph of an adoring fan. And then on for the critical product scenes, wherein it was proven that she could actually accomplish none of these things without the benefit of the rich and creamy lather of Lux Beauty Soap to repair the ravages these grueling activities caused to her otherwise flawless skin. After which she would appear radiant at a sunset dinner party on the tip-top most balcony of her Manhattan penthouse.

Ali was one of the most pleasant and genuine stars I'd run across. She'd worked in New York a few years before, and not only knew some members of our crew, she picked up on conversations with them like they were old friends. This was an unexpected plus that kept our spirits high, particularly because Harold, as always, had projected our schedule to the limits of human endurance.

"The budget, Jack, the budget," he would remind me.

The New Jersey part of the shoot slid by with no problems until late in the day, when we were set up and about to shoot the all-important product beauty shots. We'd constructed a flimsy two-wall set on one of the outside porches of the old farmhouse to look like her bathroom. Ali was there, body draped decorously in a huge bath towel, and her hair turbaned up in a smaller towel. Lighting was finally set and the cameras ready to roll, when a thunderstorm that had been building all afternoon finally broke loose, blowing down our two-wall like it was the second little piggy's house and drenching star and crew.

Nobody was hurt, and Harold went around gathering forces and cheering the troops, as efficient and capable as ever in the teeth of the winds. In fifteen minutes the worst had passed, but the set was ruined.

This was going to give us problems, as it squeezed our next day's shoot in the penthouse, a schedule which was already squeaky tight.

The penthouse Harold had selected was on 47th Street. It occupied the top three floors of a 27-story building. Everywhere one looked, there were floor-to-ceiling windows with dramatic views of the city. There was even a swimming pool, an odd, tank-like affair with a heavy plate glass window so one could watch the swimmers like fish in a bowl.

No question, the person who actually owned this place had plenty of money. The floors were marble, there was an exquisite art deco chandelier over the grand piano, and the bathroom was mirrored floor, walls and ceiling, so no matter where you looked, you saw hundreds of yourself sitting in a sleek, jet-black crapper as you fell away into infinity.

Or maybe, I thought, on closer inspection...maybe they'd once had money but had fallen on hard times...because if you looked a little closer, you could see scrapes in the gold and silver foil wallpaper. The enamel was loose on several of the piano keys. The kitchen looked like it could use a complete revamp, and even the chandelier, which proved to be of plastic rods rather than crystal, had some parts that had fallen off and were stuffed in the music bench.

No matter to Harold. With the proper lighting, a garbage dump will be made to look like a palace, and our lighting crew, used to adversity, was among the best in the city.

The owner of the penthouse wandered around as if he was in a fog. He gawked and got in the way and had to be told where to stand so he wasn't accidentally in the shots. He was my idea of a typical New Yorker--about 40, thin, wiry, unshaven, balding and wearing an expensive gold wristwatch, a 100 dollar silk dress shirt and no tie. I didn't have any idea what he did for a living or why he would put up with us coming in to disturb his life. When I asked Harold, he simply shrugged and said that people were like that. If they couldn't be in the film themselves, they wanted their place to be in films. It was the same motive that drove homeowners to whip their houses into absolutely unlivable beauty to have them photographed for House & Garden magazine.

We got right at it, and finished the re-shoot of the beauty shots the storm destroyed on the previous day, getting everything out of the way by noon. Then we set up for the patio scenes, and actually captured the canyons of New York City in those few fairyland moments between night and day when all is illusion, that brief balanced time between man-made and God-made light that Rene Magritte calls The Empire of Light. There was a moment when the world was in balance; the last light from the sun in the west, the soft candle glow from the tables on the deck on top of the penthouse and the lights from the city skyscrapers all around us in perfect harmony. At least that was the effect those New York lighting guys created. That was the reason Lux kept coming back to Harold; for the price, he gave them everything they asked for, and on top of that, the one touch more that they hadn't counted on. He'd done it with the daisy fields of Bell Canyon for Natalie Wood's shoot, and now here he was calling down God's magic for Ali MacGraw and Lux Beauty Soap.

Anyway, we got it in the can, the magic disappeared, the crew tearfully kissed and hugged Ali goodbye, and after four hours of break-down, everyone went their separate ways. Everyone except Harold and me. We still had to settle up with the owner of the penthouse.

As a producer, Harold was unique in my experience. For one thing, he always came to America with a huge stack of Travelers Checks and another of $20 bills, and a third of $100 bills. At the end of the shoot, he would settle up right then and there with the cast and crew, who worked as independent contractors.

At that time, I was in my early 30's and broad shouldered. One of my duties as American producer was to stand quietly at Harold's side and look at people if they had any problems. Not that Harold didn't pay what he owed. Quite the opposite--he always paid what he'd agreed on, exactly to the dollar.

As we came to the end of our shoot, Harold's stacks of checks and money had shrunken considerably, but he still had nearly a third of a briefcase full of money and checks. It was enough to have me worried, particularly now, because with the shoot over the owner of the penthouse had turned shrill and demanding. He pointed to an old gash in his piano, to the damaged "crystal" from his chandelier, to the scratches in his "irreplaceable" foil wallpaper. He claimed dozens of items, and angrily brought each to our attention. He was getting $3,000 for two days use of his place, but he was now claiming an additional $4,000 for damages.

Harold calmly counted out the $3,000 in cash and had the owner sign a receipt. I noticed he'd put the cash in his pocket some time earlier so he wouldn't have to open his briefcase and reveal anything of what was in there. The owner was getting louder and more angry, threatening and showing some inclination to violence, but Harold told him that if he would go through his house and write in detail the damages, we would return the next morning, look at each item and agree on the appropriate sum. Remembering how my friend Nikita Knatz used to bounce people on Steve McQueen's set, I puffed out my chest and tried to look grim. I'm sure I didn't look all that menacing with my long hair and flowing Prussian mustachios, but the owner probably didn't have his brass knuckles handy, either, and so he reluctantly agreed to Harold's proposal.

We said goodnight, and as Harold and I went down in the elevator, he was humming *Victoria, Queen of the Ocean.*

"Wow, lucky to get out of there in one piece," I said.

"Oh, it will be alright, Jack," Harold replied, as if he didn't have a care in the world.

"We're not going back there tomorrow?"

Harold gave me his gentle little smile. "Of course we are. I gave my word."

And we did show up the next morning, promptly at 10 o'clock as promised. The owner met us at the front door with an ugly smile and Sid and Lou, two pugs who looked like they could teach Niki Knatz a thing or two.

"I thought you guys might not show up," the owner said. There was an irregular line of white powder over his top lip. I'd been in show biz for a while and I could see it wasn't talcum. If Harold saw it, he didn't notice.

"Cheerio!" Harold said in his customary brisk manner. "Now why wouldn't we show? Come, come, where's the list we talked about?"

The owner hadn't started one. Harold took a yellow notepad from his briefcase, which he left open on the table. If there were any money or Travelers Checks in there, I didn't see them, and I was only looking half as hard as the three New Yorkers.

"Shall we begin?" Harold asked politely.

We walked the entire house, going room by room, with the owner pointing out every scrape, scuff and dent in the place. Harold never raised his voice, but he did debate the owner's more outrageous claims. Yet even in those moments, he always seemed to take the owner's side, contending he was going to get every penny he could for him and so it added up: $50 for the scratch on the piano, $100 for fingerprint smears on the windows, $450 to replace the scratched foil wallpaper.

After a half hour of painstaking review, the owner was running out of steam, and had only accounted for $800 worth of damages. He was also clearly out of patience.

"Okay," he finally shouted, the disgust clear in his voice. "Give me a thousand and we'll call it even."

"Eight hundred and fifty," Harold said firmly. "And I don't have the money with me. Insurance will pay you."

"Fuck that, King Arthur!" The owner roared. He looked like he was about to go berserk. "I want $1,000 and I want it now!"

He snapped his fingers and the two goons pushed me back and flanked Harold, who now looked every bit his 130 pounds.

Harold didn't bat an eye. After a very tense moment, he said, "I believe there was a scar in the elevator. Perhaps we should add that to the total."

That sounded like a good idea, so Harold snapped shut his briefcase and we all headed in that direction to investigate. Harold added another $100 for the few scrapes that had accumulated over the years in the elevator.

"You can see," he said firmly, "We have no money with us."

He pulled out his wallet, opening it to indicate the few dollar bills there. It didn't look like he was going to have cab fare back to our hotel, and he said so.

"Your only hope of getting paid," he said, "is when I submit this bill for you. And I will submit it. You have my word."

He nodded once, a brief, precise nod, and shook the owner's hand. Then he shook Sid's hand, and then Lou's.

"We must be going now," he said. He gently placed a hand on the owner's chest--and the man stepped back for him.

"Cheerio!" Harold said. And they all stepped back and watched us go. I was so relieved I didn't even mind paying the cab fare.

So the next time somebody tells you there's nothing behind the British Jack and the English Bulldog, you might do well to remember Harold Orton and to think twice about which side you join before you step in and start swinging. I know I will.

Double Billing

Inside the fabled gates of Hollywood, through which even fewer are allowed to squeeze than are able to pass through the eye of the needle, great effort is made to record the minutest details of the mighty accomplishments that are performed there. I'm speaking about deeds like writing, acting and directing. To this end, agents spend enormous bursts of outrage making sure their clients get every ounce of credits due. Top actors have to get the top billing on the newspaper ads, the posters, the TV spots, and so on: *Humphrey Bogart in The Maltese Falcon*. Great producers and brilliant directors get their name above the title: *Francis Ford Coppola's Apocalypse Now*. It is the way. What size the billing, and who goes in front of whom and on what line has destroyed many a deal that seemed like such a sure thing. Some of the greatest of the greats get double billing; for instance, Clint Eastwood when he acts and directs; or even triple billing--Oliver Stone when he writes, directs and produces.

I've never pretended to be one of the greats, though I've been hanging around the tattered edges of show business for almost three decades now. Still, odd as it sounds, I once got a double billing out of Paramount. It happened in the mid-70's on a Dustin Hoffman picture called <u>Marathon Man</u>.

The movie was based on the best-selling book of the same name by William Goldman. You may remember it; an old Nazi dentist living in the jungles of South America comes to New York for another hatful of diamonds from his safe deposit box. Through a happenstance, the old Nazi, who is played by Lawrence Olivier, comes to believe a young college student played by Dustin Hoffman is a threat to his safety.

At any rate, this all happened during the time I was working for an ad agency, Kelly/Nason West, as sort of Creative Director under office head Richard Harris. Harris was a charismatic rogue, and when he found out I'd done entertainment advertising, he started cold-calling the studios to see if he could pick up some business positioning us as *an entertainment* agency. He struck oil at Paramount; an ad-pub guy over there liked his song-and-dance, and K-N/West art director Roger Hubbard and I were given an assignment to work on Marathon Man. Roger was a terrific artist in his own right, and hoped he would be able to draw the finished poster and become rich and famous (or at least somewhat less unknown and poor). I was going to come up with a selling line for the movie--you know, the clever words near the title that are supposed to convince people to go to the theaters in droves. Fortunes are made and lost on those lines. Think it's silly? The producers of Love Story had a pleasant little tearjerker with a downer-ending until somebody came along with, "Love means never having to say you're sorry." After that, they had *a classic tale of love*, you were allowed to go to the theaters and weep, and the audience came in droves. I once did an advance trailer so filled with overpromise for Disney's The Black Hole that the theater owners sued the studio for millions of dollars. I created some compelling green-grid computer footage that sucked you along into the adventure, and I hired narrator Percy Rodriguez to intone in the booming voice of God, "Beyond life. Beyond hope. Beyond the universe. The Black Hole!" The theater owners said it was overpromise, and it was, too. If you don't believe me, you can rent a cassette of <u>The Black Hole</u> at your local Blockbuster and see for yourself.

But that's another story. Bottom line, it can be fun to do advertising for the movies. You get to hang around the studios, gaping at the stars, or being cool and ignoring them. Every film's a new project, and there's a terrific sense of anticipation as you sit down to look at the first rough cut of the picture, the work-print, as it's called.

Roger and I went over to a tiny Paramount screening room and had our look, and went back to K-N/West to do our creating. He came up with some wonderful visuals, portraits of Dustin and Lawrence powerfully intertwined, just as were their fates, and I did lots of fairly forgettable lines like, "How fast can you run, when your life is at stake?" and "Run for your life."

Our first boards were rejected by the Paramount ad-pub guy as being too small. I complained to Richard, but he said, "Give the client anything he wants. Just make sure you charge him for it." So we blew everything up giant-sized and headed back in the main gate loaded down with these huge posters mounted on foam-core. Once we got there, I found out why the blowups; we were presenting to then studio head Bob Evans, who was blind as a bat. No big deal, I'm blind as a bat too...but the story was Bob had once been an actor, and glasses didn't fit his *mystique*, or something. Nobody ever dared tell him about contacts, I suppose. I wonder what he thought people were thinking as he went around the room, holding each huge poster at arm's length and squinting at the type like he was looking at the big "E" on an eye chart. Evans looked and looked at everything we'd brought, and then he and the ad-pub guy chewed our stuff over, but it was easy to see they were marking time.

After a few minutes, Dustin Hoffman walked in. He was one of the most naturally at ease humans I've ever met. Without an ounce of pretense, he slouched into one of the couches like he owned the room, and Richard presented everything to him. Dustin seemed to like them all, but he didn't say much, just that he thought one picture Roger had drawn was nice. It was a medium shot of the actor from the waist up, half turning, looking back in alarm as he runs. Dustin got to his feet and arched an eyebrow at us. Talk about economy of expression. When nobody said anything, he left.

No more conversations about the strengths of this drawing or that line, Evans and the ad-pub guy decided *it was it.* We would use the pose in which Dustin had showed mild enthusiasm. But since Roger had used a frame of live-action footage, maybe they could just go back and use that, rather than have Roger finish his drawing (which would have cost them at least $10 grand, and, as they said, might not have the "raw realism" of the original frame). Since Dustin hadn't said anything about a line, they figured maybe they didn't need a line. That's how the poster was decided. And--fool you--you always wondered at the high debate and excruciating clarity of thinking that must go on in the top offices of the major studios.

Anyway, the Paramount ad-pub guy walked us back to our cars, telling us all the way not to be disappointed. After all, our work had resulted in the poster, hadn't it?

Roger and I went back to doing ads for Bushnell Binoculars and Esprit, *the light wine with just a touch of lime,* and I forgot all about it...until one day a few months later when Richard came roaring into my office with a huge tab from some fancy hotel in Yosemite. "That son-of-a-bitch!" he roared. "I said I would pay for a weekend! One lousy weekend! I didn't know he was going to take along his entire extended family over the Holidays! He must have bought out the hotel!"

He threw the bill on my desk like he expected me to pay it. "Damn it, if I'd known this is what the entertainment business is like, I'd never have let you talk me into it!"

It was typical Richard Harris outrage, and, as usual, had little to do with the facts. But I'd been working for King Richard for some time. These things blew over, but the key with Richard was always to face him, to point out the obvious errors in his logic. "Richard," I said, "you never even asked me. That's *your* client. You made that deal, right from the start. Remember how proud you were when you sprang it on us?"

He flew past that part like I'd never said it. But he did take the invoice off my desk. He stormed around the room for a while and then slammed himself down in the chair across from me, glaring, "How much does Paramount owe us?"

"Nothing. They paid everything."

"And you charged for every teeny-tiny little thing we did?"

"Richard, those were the fattest bills we ever sent out of here. They paid through their ears."

"Well, call him up and tell him I'm not very happy!"

"Me?!"

"Yeah, you. You work for me, so you gotta do what I say." And with that, he stormed back to his own office.

So I called over to Paramount, and the ad-pub guy listened for a moment and then said, "Hey, no problem...have we paid all your invoices yet?"

"Yeah, you have."

"How much was the last one?"

"Ahh, just over $3,000."

"Well, send it back over here again."

So I did, and in another week, they paid it again. And that's how I got a double billing out of Paramount.

It's been a long time, but still, that's the kind of thing that makes a person wonder. If they ever give me another shot, what do you think, should I go for my name above the title?

Arthur Pierson and the Lesson of the Chinese Grandmothers

You ever think you're being buried by the mountains of nits and detail work, oceans of menial tasks of all types? Sometimes I do. The impossible and contradictory directions, all the copy points, to say nothing of the mandatories and the changes. On top of that, every ad exec, marketing manager, producer, editor, magazine publisher, film director, actor and client I know thinks they're a writer and knows a better way of saying things than I do.

Some days the job bags keep coming in, piling up on my desk until it's hard to see my computer screen. And then, when I'm finally at my wit's end, strung out and yelling to the world that they've seen the last fricking piece of writing I'm ever going to do, I think of Arthur Pierson and the Chinese grandmothers.

You probably never heard of Arthur Pierson, but he was a big-time Broadway director way back in the roaring 20's until he upped his stakes and headed west to do continuity directing for the great Cecil B. DeMille. Continuity directing in the silent movies meant you had to remember who was in every scene, what they were wearing, carrying, holding and doing, what their mood was and which way they went when they left the scene.

It must have been quite a job working for CB, who was the original father of the silver screen spectacular; Arthur had to keep a running track on hordes of actors and thousands of pieces of minutia.

I met him fifty years later at Hanna-Barbera Productions under what might politely be called greatly reduced circumstances. He was sort of Bill Hanna's cleanup man on the projects Bill didn't have time for, which had to be something like picking up after Yogi Bear. Arthur didn't seem to mind, and when I met him, he was honcho-ing forty educational filmstrips through his boss's animation house. I remember there were ten strips on Ancient Civilizations that we were going to have to animate, and ten on Modern Cultures that we were sending a stills photographer around the world to capture. I can't remember the other twenty any more, but back then I was the writing supervisor on all of them, and our client, Ken Gammerman of *Look, Listen & Learn*, was giving me fits.

Ken was a revisionary maniac, and nearly every day I'd get a new sheaf of changes in the mail. Most of them seemed to be random, senseless things. Say it one way, say it another, it made no difference, and Ken never even tried to justify, he never said word one about *why* any change. And worse, about once a week he would flip-flop about what audience we were talking to. Instead of writing for 8 to 10 year olds, now he wanted to talk to 12 to 14 year olds, changes of heart that demanded major copy overhauls.

I don't think I'd have ever gotten through it without Arthur Pierson. Frail, gray and in his seventies, old Arthur would totter by and pick up all my revisions and somehow organize and have the staff type them and get them ready by the next morning. He may have been physically waning, but he had a will of steel. And yet, even at that, we were just barely staying even with the mad Gammerman.

One day I asked Arthur what kept him going, and instead of answering me directly, he invited me out to lunch. He drove his stodgy old Plymouth with his arms out straight like he was gripping the wheel of a battleship, and we somehow made it the half mile to the Far East Terrace, which was a block or so north and kitty-corner across from Universal Studios on Lankershiem Boulevard. The Far East Terrace was like a big period piece movie set from Run Run Shaw's studio in Hong Kong. You expected to see Charlie Chan stepping out from behind a lacquered screen at any minute, and the courtyard was just right for Bruce Lee to chop his way through 15 assassins before sitting down to a big spread of pressed duck and fortune cookies.

We went in and ordered a couple of dishes, and while I ranted and raved about Gammerman, Arthur turned over the fragile cups, poured green tea and gave me his distant little smile. There was a break in my ranting and he finally asked me if I liked Chinese restaurants.

"Well...sure," I replied, not quite certain what he was getting at.

"They never fail, Chinese restaurants," Arthur said. He eyed me, his pale blue eyes swimmy behind his thick, no-rim glasses. "It's because they've got a formula, a foolproof recipe. Two or three sauces, three or four kinds of meat, and a couple of big pots of vegetables. They just mix-and-match and stir it all up together back there." He waved one hand vaguely in the direction of the kitchen. "And if anything's left over, they stir it all together the next day and call it fried rice."

"Well," I shot back, still up to my ears in Gammerman and looking for something to argue about, "There's egg rolls, and that's different."

"Yes, egg rolls", he agreed pleasantly, and he shook his cup around a little bit and examined the shredded tea leaves on the bottom. "But none of that is the real secret of Chinese restaurants. The most important, deepest, darkest real secret of Chinese restaurants is Chinese grandmothers."

"What? How do you figure?"

"Well, the Chinese get twice as much meat off a chicken or a pig as anybody else, because the old ladies sit there and pick it off the bones with their fingers. It's the secret of their success."

"Chinese grandmothers?"

"Yes. It's all good meat. But imagine the patience it takes to work a chicken with your old, arthritic fingers that way, getting every last scrap. As the grandmother, she's not being paid very much, if anything at all. All of this may not seem very important to you, but it's the heart of the restaurant, where the real profit is." There was a long pause. Arthur was staring at me, and I could see that he wasn't nearly as senile as I'd thought a few bare moments before. "I'm Bill Hanna's Chinese grandmother," he said softly. "There's no shame in it. If any profit is to come from this whole Gammerman affair, we're going to have to pick the bones to find it. And I'll tell you, my young friend, you'd be surprised how much business is like that."

Looking back, I know I owe old Arthur a great deal for that insight. He gave me a broader view of what a creative person's responsibilities really are. Of course, there's nothing like the pure fun of sitting in the slipstream of your own creativity while you pour out fantastic concepts and shape them to your fondest desires. But we owe our employers and our clients-- anybody attracted to our work--much more than that. We owe them an honest, professional job, with attention having been given to every last detail. That's what finally makes our work 100% right.

That was over thirty years ago, but every now and then, when I'm upset over an assignment that's particularly knotted with addendums, legals and revisions, my mind drifts back to that lunch we had at the Far East Terrace, and I remember Arthur sharing with me the darkest secret of Chinese restaurants.

Miracles Do Happen

Ad agency head Richard Harris had positive energy flow in buckets, in bursts, in tidal waves. He was *born to lead,* and practically anybody he met gladly followed anywhere he went like poor, fated lemmings jumping off a cliff after the Pied Piper or however that old story went. A rabid womanizer and an unrepentant scamp, Richard ran both a Seattle agency with his own name on the door and an auto racing company called, appropriately enough, Redline, Inc.

The dark days for him began innocently enough when he merged his company with Kelly-Nason, a mid-sized New York agency that had put new pop in fizzled-out old products like Arm & Hammer baking soda and Ocean Spray cranberry juice through the use of focus group panels. Research-oriented advertising, the new wave of the 70's. Maybe you even remember it.

Anyway, after the merger, Richard found himself minority owner, agency head and Creative Director of offices in L.A., San Francisco and Seattle. A very busy guy. This was about 1977 and I was freelancing pretty much anything I could get--writing, producing and directing small stuff from the underbelly of Hollywood--to keep the wolf at bay. I answered an ad he placed in ADWEEK and Richard hired me as a freelance writer.

After a few hectic weeks during which I proved I was one of the world's most versatile writers (freelancers rarely have any say in their assignments, and Harris always believed in wringing the last drop of blood), he gave me a few jingles to write. Writing jingles under pressure was easy for me after surviving three years at Leo Burnett where they claimed to have invented the art form. One afternoon I did:

> *At Pic-A-Dilly*
> The smart n' the frilly
> Come out to shop every day...

The next day I wrote:

> Ah'm truckin' ma' trick ornamental tin can
> Ma' super pop-top, ma' Bizi Body Van.

Richard could see I was the Elvis of jingle writers, and with me at his command, K-N/West was going to rise through the ranks to become a multi-jillion dollar colossus. Problem was, I was picking his checkbook to pieces, raking in the dough at $50 an hour. Twelve, fourteen hours a day. And weekends. That was decent money for a freelancer in those times.

"We have to have a little talk," he said. We chewed it back and forth, and after an hour he lit up a cigar, slapped me on the back and hired me to be his new CD, a deal he regretted and reneged on fifteen minutes after I said I would.

"*Assistant* Creative Director," he said he meant, some time later. Richard was a first class charmer, but he couldn't stand it if anybody else was singing in the room. I always liked the guy--I couldn't help myself, I wasn't any more resistant to his charisma than anybody else--but as his chief rival and bottle washer, I caught a lot of abuse and so wasn't totally under his spell.

Richard loved it when we cut side-deals and produced his client's commercials outside the agency, because I did all the work and he didn't have to split his share of the profits with the guys from New York. But with every hot new idea I had, I could see he was getting a little greener.

For my part, I was more and more impatient as the months passed. I wanted to spread my wings and fly as a full-fledged Creative Director, and here was King Richard, constantly tugging at the rope around my ankles.

Things came to a head when he had to go to New York to explain to the big guys how come the West Coast wasn't producing the profits he'd promised. While he was gone, I did a quality Bushnell campaign on my own, shooting the Custom Compact binoculars on lush Persian carpets with hunting scenes on them. The client was astounded (I didn't say happy), and when he got back, Richard was justly outraged. I had given him every reason to boot me out the door.

Oddly enough, the next week he was particularly nice to me, and I would have been relieved except that the absolute true and final word filtered back through the grapevine that he'd hired a writer/art director team to replace me. How did I know for sure? The two schmucks had the bad sense to drop in and ask me where their new offices would be located. I buttonholed Richard about it the next day and he chewed his answers around like a mouthful of hot potatoes. It was a mistake, or something. I should forget it, or something. *Right. Sure, Richard.*

I made it all the way to grim Friday with Richard tiptoeing around like he didn't want to disturb the particular genius that was my *raison d'etre*. I could understand his not wanting to fire me and then having to pay me through Friday. Times were tough all over.

But first thing Friday morning, he came in howling like a banshee. There were four or five K-N employees sitting around the main conference room when he started hammering me. *I was a klutz. I was a moron. I was an advertising retard.* The others didn't leave the room, but they quickly and quietly put a little space between themselves and me.

I just looked at Richard like he was crazy. I didn't say a word. I could see that he hoped I would quit so he wouldn't have to fire me and pay the extra two-weeks' wages. Things were really tough, Richard. In my world, too. My silence made him madder and madder until he was nearly frothing. *Hey, wasn't I a man? What did he have to do to make me stand up and be offended?* As he worked himself up toward the crescendo of his little one-act play, the private phone started ringing in his office. I could see it was irritating him, but it wasn't on a line the receptionist could get to. It rang and rang until he finally broke off in raging mid-sentence and stomped out to answer it. The other people in the room just sat there, breathing softly and looking off into space.

The minutes ticked by, and we could hear bits and snatches of Richard's voice rising and falling in the next room. It was a long call, nearly a half hour, and the Richard who rejoined us in the conference room was a sadly different man. His face actually sagged, and he had a tic in his right eye. Napoleon after Waterloo. He slumped in his chair and gave me a look that said our private war was over.

"That was New York", he said. "I've been fired." He wandered out to the reception room, hands stuffed in his pockets. He looked suddenly old, like one of those vampires who aren't getting enough fresh blood.

I stayed on at K-N/West for another two years after he left, and then I switched jobs and had a long run doing entertainment advertising as the Creative Director at Disney Studios. Without Richard in the way, I got the client experience I so desperately needed, and learned to *hit the target*, as they say. In short, I became a real Creative Director.

But I tell you, it was a narrow squeak. A couple of minutes one way or the other on one of the grimmest

Fridays I've ever lived through, and none of that would have happened. So don't tell me there's no such thing as miracles.

Billy and the Sorcerer

The Hollywood process of making film and TV shows is in some respects similar to that of a factory. There is a constant need for new movies and television shows, and so there are production lines that have been established to handle that demand. Just as different people will want SUV's, vans, sports cars or pickup trucks, different sorts of moviegoers will want action pictures, chick flicks, family fare, and viewers parked in front of their television sets will want cop shows, comedy, horror, reality TV, the shopping channels, travel channels, news channels, and so on.

Enterprises that manufacture goods and services are limited by financial considerations. In other words, most ordinary people wouldn't even dream of starting up a car company or a soft drink manufacturing plant, simply because they don't have the resources. Yes, there are always a few dreamers who will be driven to build a better automobile or invent a more desirable brand of Coca-Cola. However, when it comes to telling stories and making movies, it seems there is some sizeable percentage of the population that is ready and eager to plunge in, not realizing how cold, dark and deep the waters can actually be. All this to say that, if you must write the Great American Novel or produce the next big box office winner, it's not a bad idea to read up on just how to do it. Film schools and writing classes are great, but if you don't have the time, you actually can learn-it-yourself by reading the right books and taking small but bold steps before taking out that second mortgage and betting the farm on your great idea.

Here are several works that I've found invaluable: The Art of the Novel, by Milan Kundera. Story, by Robert McKee. On Writing, by Stephen King. The Art of Dramatic Writing, by Lajos Egri. How To Write A Screenplay That Sells To Hollywood, by Syd Field. Screenwriting Workshop, also by Syd Field. How To Market You & Your Book, By Richard F.X. O'Connor. The Golden Goblet Newsletter, by Marilyn Peake. How to Get Happily Published, by Judith Appelbaum.

Beyond textbook and school learning, you can do well to connect with any club or group that cultivates writing. I personally like Francis Ford Coppola's website, http://www.zoetrope.com , where you can post your work and have it reviewed in return for your comments on other scripts, short stories or poetry. Other helpful sites to put you in contact with writers and producers are http://www.writers.net and http://www.thenextbigwriter.com .

If you're a person of the female persuasion, you might want to read Not One of the Boys by Brenda Feigen, so long as you counterbalance it with Gerry Spence's How to Argue and Win Every Time.

Books like these, collections of memoirs written by or about people who have survived in the creative jungles and wildernesses of the world, can be helpful so long as you use them as background and don't rely on them as bibles. Success stories are wonderful; but I think, if you know enough about what actually happened, you can learn nearly as much from the failed projects of talented people as you can from their successes. And one last thought to mull: being a successful storyteller is one of the hardest things in the world, otherwise why would practically any novelist or filmmaker have a disaster or two in addition to their greatest work? Which brings us to Billy Friedkin and his spectacularly failed movie Sorcerer.

I guess maybe if you asked the average American moviegoer to name the top Hollywood filmmakers--people, not studios--most would say Steven Spielberg at the very top of the list followed by a handful of others. Ronnie Howard. Mel Gibson, maybe. Clint Eastwood. Kevin Costner. Maybe Barbra Streisand. But, chances are, nobody will mention William Friedkin. How soon we forget here in Hollywoodland, where hope and dreams and careers fade nearly as fast as they bloom. They don't call it *lotusland* for nothing. There was a time after William Friedkin had made The French Connection and The Exorcist when he ranked right up there with the legends.

Now, although the Friedkin pictures had made piles of money, there is another matter that tugs at the souls of filmmakers, and that is the artistic merit of their efforts. It will come as no surprise that European critics by and large scoff at American cinematic efforts as formulaic, soulless and hence, without merit. Billy's pictures, at the time, were considered prime examples.

You may want to know, American filmmakers respond by calling most European flicks boring, tedious and crushingly dull. And so it goes. In literature, when a boy and a girl of opposing cultures meet, the results are briefly sweet, followed by tragic consequences. Romeo & Juliet. West Side Story. Tea and Sympathy...well, maybe not Tea and Sympathy, but you get the idea. This unpleasant story trend began to be played out in real life when William Friedkin married actress Jeanne Moreau, high priestess of the European art of the cinema.

Sorcerer was a remake of a powerful and artistically successful film called Wages of Fear, or however you say that in French. It had originally been shot in French and later dubbed in English, an existentialist story of desperate men in desperate times. Now <u>The Exorcist</u> had done so well, they brought the devil back for two return engagements where he pulled in dwindling but still mighty box office numbers. All well and good; but since <u>The French Connection</u>, the bloom had pretty much been off Billy's rose. <u>Sorcerer</u> was going to change all that, and something more--it was going to show his wife and maybe the rest of the world that Billy knew art as well as dollar signs.

All well and good, but there was real money on the table, and the Hollywood moneymen, the critics, the trades, the flacks and the pundits weren't so sure. If <u>Sorcerer</u> was going to be as innovative as Friedkin promised, it wouldn't hurt to go a little out of the box and hire some guys who weren't intimidated by *different and unusual*. And so it was that, at the bidding of the marketing gurus at Paramount, art director Roger Hubbard and I showed up on the doorstep of Billy's office.

I guess it isn't giving away any trade secrets to reveal--in case you saw the picture and missed the point--that <u>Sorcerer</u> is actually one of several trucks used by several of the doomed protagonists to transport some old and unstable dynamite. The name is only seen in a flash-cut about halfway through the picture (they even cut it out of some versions). Nobody mentions the name in the dialogue, and this truck is the one that doesn't make it through, being blown up along the way. Somewhere, the ghosts of long-dead French filmgoers flick their cigarettes and cast sad eyes at the horizon. Film, like life, is indeed little more than a jest.

Well, in this case making a great film wasn't our job; we'd been hired to sell the turkey, to promote the dog, to con fools into showing up at theaters across this great cinema-loving land of ours. Roger and I saw the first rough cut of the picture while sitting on film cases in a cramped little screening room over at Universal. (This was a Paramount/Universal co-venture. It's a sign of sinking confidence when the moneymen start hedging their bets, a little like a Vegas gambler reviewing his recent play and then taking out insurance at the blackjack table.) The way we viewed it, the picture was over three hours long. It was a wandering tale that tried to follow the lives of five men we never get to know or like as they commit various misdeeds and are sentenced to brutal slave-worker conditions somewhere in tropical Central America. Of course, this being *European influenced cinema art*, fate deals them one final chance to redeem themselves, a desperate chance that proves to be little more than an illusion.

While I was an original out-of-the-box thinker, Roger, who was a fine artist in his own right, was more interested in doing finished art for the poster, which would be financially rewarding and help make his career as well. Somehow, against his protestations and reservations, I convinced him to work with me on concepts that were in the grand continental tradition, weighted with their own heavy significance and with philosophic importance. The visuals were largely of giant broken granite statues half-buried in the sand, which stretched away into the distance like a Daliesque dream of Shelley's poem Ozymandias. I thought of it as European Zen, the stuff of surrealism, much like the film itself, presenting questions without answers. I wrote appropriately lurid lines (for counterpoint, I told Roger), lines like *With Fear for a Bride, and Death alongside...*We had Magritte, Shelley and Klawitter. How could Friedkin resist?

I must say, Roger outdid himself. His broken statues asked all the right questions in all the right places. He even designed an alphabet, a red-blood dripping word, <u>Sorcerer</u>, the set of letters copyrighted and to be used only for marketing the picture. (This actually started a little run of copycat designs, and for a few years, nearly every suspense, sci-fi and horror flick tried to emulate his success with their own logo design.)

I remember going over to the studio and waiting in the outer room for our audience with Billy. There was a lot of shouting in the inner chambers. Perhaps I was imagining things, but I felt the air was heavy with fear, disgust and dismay. Roger looked at me, but as the fearless leader I knew I could show no weakness. I put my feet up on Friedkin's coffee table and pretended to be interested in a copy of Metal Hurlant, the blood-and-sex version of Heavy Metal in the original French.

Roger eyed me nervously, and I gave him a wink.

"Be careful, Rog," I said. "Fear is contagious."

"So is stupidity," he said, giving me his best *you-are-such-a-dick-head* glare.

Friedkin came out to look over our little offering. He wasn't as old as I expected, even after the somewhat juvenile commotion I'd overheard coming from his office. I thought he looked like a young Jewish doctor who'd lately been in a snarly miff over some dog poop on his wing tips. Of course I didn't say so.

The great man blankly studied the poster comps while I went into my patter about high art and European Zen. As I spoke, I could see great question marks forming in the fog over his head. While he didn't spit on anything, I believe it safe to say Magritte didn't click on any switches in his brain. With a few harsh words, he sent Roger and me away to do posters of big, battered trucks with menacing steel-grill teeth bumping across perilous and slippery bridges.

On our way out, Roger gave me his best *I-told-you-so, dick-head* look. I didn't say anything. I figured I deserved it.

A few months later, I saw the final cut of Sorcerer. It was down around 110 minutes, as I recall. That's about where the theater owners prefer them, so they can rotate the cattle and sell more Cokes, popcorn and hot dogs--the syrup trade, they call it.

Although the picture itself went by a lot faster, now it felt choppy and alienating. I still couldn't get much of an idea what it was all about. And I was starting to suspect Friedkin didn't know either. Maybe Roger was right, after all. Maybe ignorance was catching.

He's Back in the 3rd Row Under K-4

Today, Disney is again at the top of the heap, so you may not remember that things were not always so. There was a grim and dismal time when the name had lost its luster and no longer cast magic upon the silver screen.

Let me remind you of the late 70's, of those days when a mighty scourge was upon the studio. The decade of lean box office years had come and gone, and still the till was dry and parched. Plagues of critics were in the air, darkening the afternoon sky and the pestilence of unemployment was everywhere at hand. All those who worked the lot of The Mouse and The Duck, from the pleasant old ink-and-paint ladies who fattened the cats for the coyotes that prowled the northern berm to the gnarled keeper of the film vaults, knew the pretenders who had stolen Walt's jeweled thinking crown and his enchanted drawing scepter had never been able to make the crown or the scepter spit forth fire as had done the master.

Still, one must step back, if only for a moment, and wonder how it truly was in those days of yore; it couldn't have been easy for this batch of Walter-Wanna-be's after the studio genius had made his premature and unexpected departure. Everywhere these unlucky yokels turned, there was something else The Old Man had done, making their best ideas look like dog turds. Pinocchio, for Jiminy's Sake, how did the Old Man get that damn bug so--so *right?!* You've got to be a touch sympathetic. Pete's Dragon, after all, would have been a decent enough little film in its own right, if everyone wasn't always comparing it to the pure filmic wonder of Mary Poppins.

By the time I got to the lot in 1979, Walt had been dead a while, and the pretenders had given up on some of their more lofty goals. No more of this *Let's do Walt one proud* stuff. Like junkies on a fix, they were pouring out crap movie after crap movie, still hoping to rub the magic beads the right way and somehow cause the lightning to strike. Take Down. Unidentified Flying Oddball. Herbie Goes Bananas. The Last Flight of Noah's Ark. Midnight Madness. Condorman. The Devil and Max Devlin. The Watcher in the Woods. The Black Hole. The list goes on and on, and reading it, you know that these had to be desperate men.

There were a good many disillusioned craftsmen hanging on at the lot in those days, finding themselves not unlike belabored serfs looking upward to wipe the sweat from their brow only to see the magic castle overtaken by mutant dwarves and troll mercenaries. In the face of all this filmic waste and decay, they could only dream of the Golden Age of Walt and hope a bolt of inspiration would strike somebody--*anybody*--in what many of them thought of as the regime of the fool and the jester. They would gather around the old boiler room deep under the Animation Building and huddle in little corners of the cafeteria to tell their treasured old Walt stories, almost as if conjuring his memory would bring him back in the flesh. *I remember the time Walt did this...Say, do ya remember the time Walt was out at the park...Walt never would have done it this way...Walt would have been furious if he'd-a seen that footage. No lie, Walt would-a fixed that!*

The mood was unremittingly gloomy. Some of the latter-day Post-Waltian movies were so bad that the old projectionists claimed they gagged while trying to eat their lunches. A few comments like that and pretty soon word was all over the lot that Disney had another dog picture--not dog as in <u>Old Yeller</u>, dog like in *pooper-scooper*.

Then the top guys would charge around, fuming and trying to stem the flood of shop talk that *Yea, indeed, the new movie stinketh badly* before word got out to the trades. I could never figure out why they cared about that. <u>Variety</u> and <u>The Hollywood Reporter</u> wouldn't print it anyway--they only printed newsworthy stuff and it was no longer news that Disney was producing box office bombs on a regular basis.

I also don't know where the rumor started that these same studio heads had Walt cryonically frozen and buried in a secret vault somewhere under the parking lot. I never found anybody who would admit it, but you know how, in villainous times such as those, stories like that get their start.

The way the apocryphal and banished tale goes is that, on certain moonlit nights, when the humidity and the temperature are both just right, a haze will form over the secret sacred spot. Sometimes it is a haze, and sometimes a rectangular rim of frost on the asphalt; and on the rarest occasions--say, the 55th anniversary of one of the parks or Mickey's 100th birthday--it will be St. Elmo's fire.

On the other hand, I do confess to creating the bizarre Busby Berkeley number featuring a bunch of top Disney execs all dancing and bowing around the steaming ice-glazed crypt while they sing:

> We're gonna bring you Walt
> We've got him in the vault
> Ideas all intact

We know how you'll react
Long as the glass don't crack.

At this point in the number the execs break into a combination, throwing their hands right-left-right like a shu-be-doo and alternating with the old bees knees, and finally they do the shuffle-off-to-Buffalo and as a last touch, the Keep on Truckin'...

See ya later, Animator!
Mighty Prestidigitator!

As they exit, they are replaced with a sad group of hunchback Disney creatives. As these fellows lurch their spastic way up to the crypt to wail the next few lines with a sad, dirge-like effect, the whole cryonic thing mechanically tilts up through the use of hydraulic pumps, and we see the faint image of someone inside the frosted glass. His arms are outstretched with dark clamps on his hands. There are tubes in his arms, and the electrode wires around his head have the effect of a crown of thorns. The hunched writers, producers and directors sing:

We're gonna bring you Walter
Nailed high above the altar
Brainwaves of pure lucre
Ideas super-duper
To bring us from our stupor

As the creatives hobble, crawl and moonwalk away from their fallen master, they beg for one last idea:

See ya later, Animator
Mighty Prestidigitator!

It was all part of a Broadway stage musical I wanted to do, using some of the bushel baskets of money that were coming in from Disneyland and Disney World, just a little something-project to keep away the worms and madness wrought from working on all those rotten flicks. Maybe it was a touch sacrilegious. Still, I doubt if Jesus would have minded half as much as Walt's lawyers.

Be that as it may, back in the real, sad world that was the Disney studio in those days; when the pretenders couldn't get the crown or the scepter to work, they spent a lot of time on the final stage of their production projects, the stage where they blamed the innocent. They blamed the continuing lackluster performance of their movies on the shifting tastes of the American public. They cited demographics that showed there were less people alive who went to the movies, studies that proved less people liked the movies, and statistics that indicated the American movie-going family was no longer an entity. They blamed it on their own producers for not coming up with great scripts. And on the Hollywood community for not giving them the respect they deserved. On the movie owners, for letting their theaters get shabby and thinning the syrup in their Cokes. On the top-line stars, who shunned parts in Disney movies like the plague. On their own casting department, that couldn't convince these disrespectful stars to change their minds. On their directors, for directing things poorly; on their cameramen, for not keeping it in focus; on their editors, for not cutting the film right; on their projectionists, for not projecting it right; on their publicity people, for not understanding the greatness of their efforts and so not communicating it to the American people. For all I know, they may even have blamed it on Walt, for not getting back to them from under the parking lot. But they never, ever blamed it on themselves.

It goes without saying, Disney wasn't really a fun place to be around in those days. No wonder Walt never came out to play. But if you ever want to see him for yourselves, you'll have to bring a set of those ropes with anchor hooks on the end like they use in the old pirate movies. Pick a dark and stormy night and try scaling the wall on the back side of the lot, halfway around from the front entrance. Set your compass for the southwest and cut diagonally across the studio, heading for the old parking lot. He's back in the third row under K-4. Look

or the magic wisps. Even after all this time, you won't
have any trouble finding it.

144

The Man Who Married Snow White

They did a movie about it not too long ago. The blurbs screamed *Holly Wood if she could.* Kim Basinger starred as the world's sexiest line drawing, a cartoon bombshell who wants to become a real person, only there are laws against it. The laws were put there for good reason; in real life, it never works out between toons and humans.

Walt Disney knew this, or at least suspected as much, way back when he was working on the world's first animated movie. Uncle Walter may not have been the absolute guru-level genius that today's Corporate Disney would like you to believe, but on the other hand, you didn't have to be a wizard to recognize the problem. Artists, you see, tend to be a lusty, wild, imaginative bunch of rascals. Look at Van Gogh, cutting off his own ear, and Gauguin leaving those who loved him and running halfway around the world to paint naked tropical ladies, and even staid Andy Wyeth proving to be our modern-day Lothario, endlessly slapping up his canvas stack of Brunhilda fantasies.

Walt's problem wasn't just lascivious artists; to create the world's finest animation, you couldn't ever fake it. You needed real talent, and when they drew, they had to do so from real life. In other words, artists

145

were going to have to come in contact with live flesh here. Walt knew this. So when he got down to the brass nuts of reworking the old fairy tale, after carefully clearing the rights with the Brothers Grimm and Mother Goose, he began a search for a real-life model who would inspire his band of merry men to draw their hearts out. She had to be a marvel, a wonder, an ecstasy--in short, the fairest of them all.

Having no glass slipper for a clue, he was somewhat at a disadvantage. But nothing ever stopped Walt--just read the approved biographies if you suspect I jest--and after searching appropriately in the darkest corners of the land, he came up with a young, teenaged girl named Marge. She was bright and winsome and she had a smile that sent the butterflies, the mice and the birds skipping about at the required velocity. Her slender grace radiated beauty. Yes, perhaps Kim was sexier, but Marge had that *je ne sais quoi* that went beyond mere high octane lust into the realm of pure heavenly attraction. In short, she was the kind of girl you wanted to bring home to mother, and then take straight off to bed.

Naturally, those roguish animators immediately fell in love with her. And one of them, the handsome and clever young Art Babbitt, carried on perhaps more playful mischief with her than any of the rest. Or, who knows, maybe it was just that he had the heavy responsibility of animating the young grace, and so was with her for many, many long hours throughout the day and night. The picture itself proceeded slowly, and while poor Uncle Walt was out beating the streets for more filthy lucre to keep his doors open, there was much time for dalliance in between the frames.

Things being what they are twixt toons and people, Art soon became infatuated with every curve of her rapture, as the old books are wont to put it. And, to make a long story short, he defied the conventions of the times, the dire warnings of his good friends and the

TINSEL WILDERNESS

wrath of He-Who-Had-His-Name-Above-The-Title--and married her.

You can imagine this did nothing at all to please Uncle Walter, for he had his entire career, to say nothing of an enormous fortune, wrapped up in this picture, which was at best a highly experimental enterprise for that day and age. Marge *couldn't* be off somewhere in Sunland, California having babies; Snow White had to be touring all over the country, presiding over the grand openings in her flowing hair and puff-sleeved gown. But Art and Marge had done what they had done. She would now try to combine the best of both worlds, dividing her time between domestic tranquility and barnstorming America to save the studio.

It was during this troubled and eventful period that the reasons for the great law barring human relations with toons became apparent. Wonder of wonders! Marge in real life wasn't at all like the gentle, wise and kind Snow White of Art's illusion. She was a typical gum-cracking, short-tempered, know-next-to-nothing teenage kid. Maybe even brat would apply. Art went along on the tour, but the pace was torrid and it wasn't much fun. Living with the princess, who had her own mind and priorities, was proving far more difficult than drawing her gaily dancing as she swept up around the cottage and singing as she stirred the porridge for her surly little men. And worse, all this fairyland fame was going to her pretty little head. Art felt he was seeing less and less of her. It was Walt's fault--he was driving them apart! It was Marge's fault--she couldn't see what Walt was doing to her! It was his own fault--why hadn't he seen she was just a teenaged monster?! It was the fault of the business--nobody should have to go through the grueling schedule they did!

In all fairness, Marge couldn't be everywhere and everybody they wanted her to be at the same time. Nobody could have. And, if her head did get turned a bit, was she to blame? After all, everybody gets married

and settles down, sooner or later, but how many
maidens dance and sing with dwarves and wake up to
the kiss of the world's handsomest prince? So Marge
and Arthur broke up, and Snow White ran off and
married Gower Champion, who was a dancer and sort of
a prince, or at least famous, in his own right.

There were a lot of reasons Walt Disney didn't like
Art Babbitt. For one thing, Art was very big in the labor
movement at the studio. Walt was never easy with a
buck, and in those early years Art fought him tooth and
nail to get a fair shake for all the little people who spent
endless hours on the huge amount of drudgery it takes
to make an animated movie. In so doing, Snow White's
ex proved to be a very big thorn in Walt's side for quite a
while, until the young animator went off to serve in World
War II. Even then it wasn't over, and after V-J Day
Babbitt sued Walt to come back to the studio and claim
his old job. As there was a clear law about it, and Art
insisted on his rights, Walt had to give in. Art showed up
for work each day and claimed his check at the end of
each pay period. But nothing in the very clear law said
Walt had to give him real work, and so Art sat alone at
the shabby desk in the small, empty office they provided
for him, doing absolutely nothing. And no one Walt hired
at the studio, from Art's closest friends down to the lowly
shoeshine boy, dared to speak a word to him.

A lot of bitterness, over a lot of things. But years
later, when Art worked with me at Hanna-Barbera, he
told me that he'd finally figured it out. Although his
struggle to unionize Disney was a part of it, he was
convinced that his difficulties with the old man all
stemmed from his decision to break the rules and marry
pretty little Snow White.

"You can mess with the proverbial boss's
daughter," Art said with a rueful grin, "just don't ever fool
around with his creation."

The Santa Claus Murders

I once was a major part of *a family happening* that I thought was really funny, at least in retrospect, but nobody else laughed at all. In fact, my wife never quite forgave me. To this day she still questions my sense of humor, and she will relate this one particular incident to prove her point.

It happened when my eldest son Jason, who's now a grown man and a lawyer, was only three or maybe four years old. It was a month or two before Christmas, and, I suppose, visions of sugarplums were already dancing in the young lad's head. My wife and I sat reading the Sunday paper while he played and slurped away at his breakfast.

Suddenly, without really knowing why, I muttered from behind the paper as if reading an interesting headline out loud to myself, "Huh. SANTA HIT BY 747." I continued reading, "While test-riding his new sleigh in poor visibility yesterday, Santa was struck down by a jet passenger plane on a polar flight to Europe. Rudolph is in critical condition and is not expected to pull through. Santa is survived by Mrs. Claus and about a thousand unnamed dwarf toy-makers...what do you know about that?" I turned the page without looking out from behind the paper.

"Oh, Jack, don't be silly," my wife said reprovingly. My son said nothing.

I continued to turn the pages, looking for the sports news. My wife went back to the Calendar Section, trying to figure out what movie we were going to see that afternoon. About 30 or 40 seconds went by, and finally the rustle of the pages and the long silence were punctured by a grief-stricken howl of kiddie horror.

I was so startled I dropped the paper. I'd actually forgotten what I'd said, and was wondering if Jason had seen cookie monster's evil brother or if an alligator had bitten off his foot.

"NOW see what you've done," my wife snarled, looking at me as if I'd strangled the puppy as she rushed to her baby's side.

I'm always amused when I remember that domestic scene, though over the years she has never quite forgiven me. Yet, no matter how bad it makes me look, I don't seem to care when she takes me to task for that evil deed. Somehow the memory and the way she talks about it only make it funnier.

I always felt the loner in this, as if perhaps there was something dark and sinister in my character that could make me chuckle at the misfortune of an innocent...until I talked with Ward Kimball, and he set me straight on Santa Claus.

Ward was one of the original "9 old men" of Disney who saved Walt's *derriere* when he was about to go broke on the unfinished <u>Snow White and the Seven Dwarves</u>. A week or so ago, he was telling me about some of the high jinks that took place at the studio in the old days, complaining that nobody could seem to get right anymore the way things actually happened.

"They are <u>history</u>, you know," Ward said good-naturedly enough, implying that they were open to anybody's interpretation. "For instance," he continued, "everybody's always getting the story of me and the gorilla suit all wrong."

"Well, why don't you tell me the real story, Ward?"

"Okay...it was a thing I was supposed to do for my youngest daughter Chloe, who was three or four at the time. My wife wanted me to do Santa. You see, my two other kids were a little older, and I'd been Santa for them, and for the other kids their age in the neighborhood. I had this suit and the beard--the works-- and we had this big chimney in our living room. The other grown-ups would gather the kids, and at the appropriate time somebody'd distract them by saying they heard a noise or something, and I'd slip away and put on the Santa suit. And then somebody else would hear a jingle or something in the right direction, and the kids would rush into the living room where I'd step out of the chimney with a big bag. All the kids would get some little gift and I'd give contraceptives to the parents.

"Well, I'd always prided myself that none of the children ever knew it was me; but my two other kids were older now, I figured they knew about Santa. I told my wife that I wasn't going to do it anymore, but she didn't believe me. Without me agreeing, she got out the old Santa suit and had it repaired and cleaned, ready for the grand appearance.

"On the day when I was supposed to be Santa, I stopped off at Western Costume and rented a gorilla suit on my way in to the studio. It was quite a nice suit, very realistic and all. I wore it around Disney and had a lot of fun in the elevators and chasing the girls up and down the halls. I even wore it on the way home. I got a ride from a friend of mine who had a little tan convertible with right-hand drive; you know, with the steering wheel on the right like they do in England.

"Well, that was fun, too. People would look over and see a gorilla sitting in the little car next to them, and they'd do a start. And then they'd think the gorilla was driving because of the right-hand steering wheel, and they'd do another take and we must have been responsible for eight or nine cars driving right off the road or into each other.

"Anyway, I hid the outfit next door before we got home. And when the great moment came and we did the business, all the little kiddies came into the room expecting Santa, but this time I was a gorilla. They toddled in expecting treats and instead a great, hairy, growling animal stepped out of the fireplace. Poor little Chloe!

"In a second, the room was a panic. The cat jumped four feet straight up, legs and hair out, and started tearing around the room the way they do. We had a Dalmatian at that time, and he started running circles around me, barking and trying to get his teeth into me. The little kids were all upset--yelling and screaming and in tears.

"It was all over in a minute. I saw right away I'd made a mistake. I had time for a few hops and a few mean growls and I headed out the front door in full retreat with the room in an absolute shambles and the damn spotted dog nipping at my behind. I don't think they ever forgave me.

"I was out of the house, but I wasn't out of hot water yet. Robert Peak and some of the other artists from the studio had called the police and alerted them that a dangerous pet gorilla had escaped from this animal farm that used to be in Thousand Oaks. Robert told them the gorilla was dangerous and had to be treated with extreme care--and he gave the location of the few blocks around my house as where the beast had last been seen. So while I was running over next door to get rid of the gorilla suit, there was a squad car patrolling the neighborhood looking for me, and it's just sheer luck that I didn't get shot or trapped in a big net and dragged away."

I must confess, since hearing Ward's story, I've become incorrigible. I don't worry about my sense of humor anymore, no matter how warped my wife or anybody else says it is. If I see something and it amuses me, I just go ahead and laugh. Why not? After all, if Ward Kimball and I could both bump off Santa Claus and find something amusing about it, the world indeed must be a very funny place.

A Picture's Worth a Thousand Words, After All...

After the army, I started my professional career as a cub copywriter. So I guess it was only natural that, when I was presenting a new idea in the years that followed, I made a big fuss over the words first...even if I had an image in mind. As the years went by, I gradually came to realize the validity of people who thought visually, and I began to try to emulate them as part of my own creative process. Yet, even after I became a film director and joined the DGA, in some strange way I thought all "real creative people" used words with the same high degree of importance.

It was the early 1980's. I was at Disney and we were working on a picture called <u>The Watcher in the Woods</u>, an attempt to do a scary picture with a somewhat confused script adapted from a terrific YA novel by Florence Engel Randall. As had happened several times before at the studio while I was there, they had nearly completed production (what is known as principle photography) when everybody involved realized they didn't have an ending.

At that time my title was Creative Director of Motion Picture & Broadcast Something, Something, Something, I can't even remember...but the operating notion is that the longer your title the narrower and more restricted your ability to get things done. When a picture got in trouble like this, my boss Bob King, the head of Publicity, would ask us--the writer/producers, the PR people, internal writers, flacks, petty bosses (like me), etc.--to come up with ideas to help out the production team, and we would do so in spite of the fact that Ron Miller, the studio head of production, resented it and we would uniformly get our heads kicked in for daring to presume.

Anyway, Tom Leetch, the producer of Watcher in the Woods, didn't seem to be a really bad guy, and so in short order we were all churning out ideas and looking forward to screen credits and stories in the Hollywood Reporter about how we'd saved Watcher.

The meeting started on a mean level and sagged towards nasty. Tom was frustrated and angry with his production problems and felt humiliated that the publicity nerds had been called in. Not in what I'd call a favorable listening mood for the home team.

I had my own ideas about what was wrong with Watcher, and so when my turn came I passed around a few pages outlining how I thought we could "fix" the picture. The first thing I saw was that when the alien creature appeared, he was a glowing, snot-green colored mass of something. In the book, the creature is a "good" though enormously powerful (and inadvertently dangerous) being who is simply trapped in some sort of space-time locker (in an old tree) and can't get out. Tom and his assistants nodded, yawned and looked out the window while I suggested blue might be more appropriate. I went on, explaining the script didn't really "get" the book, and their interpretation was just a cheap horror shot (I was more polite than I'm saying, here.) and if they wanted the movie to make sense they had to get a little closer to the book which was as much sci-fi as it was horror. There were more yawns and one instance of covert nose-picking.

Clearly having made no impact, I settled in my seat as Harrison Ellenshaw, Jr. rose to address the meeting. Harrison was the quasi-famous art director son of a famous art director dad. I think Tom had invited him as sort of a secret weapon, his antidote for meddling publicity people who thought they could do films. Harrison nodded to the two assistant producers and they turned around two huge cork boards that were resting against a back wall. On these were mounted a series of scenes.

Harrison had done everything exactly opposite from what I personally believe was the way to go. He had an even more violent yellow-green to his snot-spray monster, and also had it appear in a glowing chartreuse lobster-like manifestation, like some radioactive crawler from the deep floating mysteriously in the air.

But Tom and his boys had perked up. I could see their eyes were glowing as Harrison blathered on about how big and scary things were going to be. Perhaps there was hope for this picture after all. Perhaps they wouldn't have to re-fi their homes, perhaps they wouldn't be laughed out of town.

I'd seen him around the studio on <u>The Black Hole</u>, and in my opinion, Harrison wasn't much of a wrist, but his wild scribbles didn't have to be good art--they were conveying action. There wasn't a word of dialogue or description in his entire presentation, BUT HE WAS TALKING THEIR LANGUAGE THROUGH PICTURES.

Now be warned--I'm not saying pictures are The Golden Path. Harrison may have had the studio by the cahones, but his problem was, he was unwittingly leading them down a very bad path, and within weeks things turned outright ugly. The monster was very time-consuming and expensive to film, and never did look anything more than odd. Then too, Harrison sold them on additional "other-world" footage with strange planets and weird otherly worlds that seemed to have nothing to do with the original story. One more production note:

they had to call back a blond actress who had dyed her hair dark for another project, and in the process of re-blonding, they had fried her hair so badly it came out in handfuls...so the poor girl had to play her scenes with an obvious, lumpy blond wig.

All that badness, and yet I think that experience finally converted me. For the first time I realized that there were mature Hollywood producers, and even studio heads, who actually could not visualize what a scene might look like simply from reading the script. The words, no matter how brilliant, weren't enough. They had to see the pictures. A good learning experience for me...but not so good for the studio.

Convinced they had the picture back on the right track and that this was a true horror picture, the scariest that Walt Disney Studios had ever done, they decided to open the picture in New York City, a very tough movie-going town that had not been very kind to our pictures in the past. Distribution had us do huge ads warning "Too Scary To Bring The Family--Better Leave The Little Kids at Home".

New York City took us at our word...Watcher opened on a Friday night and only a handful of people attended. Unfortunately, one of them was Vincent Canby, the notorious, sharp-tongued film critic who wrote that Watcher In The Woods had limped into town "...with an unfortunate, crustacean-like monster looking like a refugee from a Chinese New Years parade..."

And They Go Beep-Beep

Bugs Bunny and all his friends--Tweedy Bird, Porky Pig, Daffy Duck, Wile E. Coyote, The Road Runner, and so on--had been around too long. At least, that was the network perception. I don't know how the network programmers came to this conclusion at this particular point in time; after all, every single cartoon came from the same old Warner Brothers library and had been rotated many, many times into the one hour show that had run every Saturday morning since the birth of time. But then, I've never been able to understand why those guys do anything they do. But I knew enough to recognize dangerous times in the tinsel wasteland.

If you're responsible for a show in dark days like that, you hang onto the family jewels and hope the bullet doesn't have your name on it. The Bugs Bunny Show was (and is) what they call "a paste-up" show, essentially "classic" old cartoons that had originally been made to run as movie shorts. After a while, you start to run out of ways to combine the various cartoons. At that point, there's only one other thing you can do--put a new wrapping on the package.

A few years before, I'd done the same thing for Disney, designing a new opening, bumpers and close for the hoary old <u>Wonderful World of Disney</u> which had run for over 20 years on Sunday Night. I wrote lyrics for a song "Welcome To Disney's Wonderful World", John Debney (Old Lou's son) wrote the music, and I had John David Moore build sequences chock-full of the most magical moments from the enormous film vaults of Disney. (In fact, I'm still getting residuals from that song. Just recently, I picked up $2.80 from Venezuela, and last year I got nearly $12 from Italy, Spain and Finland.) Now Warner Brothers was calling and asking me to do the same thing for Bugs.

The old opening featured Bugs and his pals in tuxes, tails and canes doing a sort of Fred Astaire routine in front of the spotlights to an upbeat razz-matazz show-biz opening. Their new idea was to call the show "The Bugs Bunny/Road Runner Show", give it a new opening, bumpers and close, and run essentially the same old stuff in the middle, though each show would be sure to feature a Bugs Cartoon and a Road Runner cartoon. It all sounded familiar to me; but then, if those guys didn't think the way they do, guys like me wouldn't be so much in demand.

I drove over to Burbank for a meeting with Steven Greene, who was the Warner's Animation creative mogul at that time. Greene didn't know what he wanted, but he was a real experimenter, and thought maybe we could do something "cool" or "really wild"--something on the frontiers of animation--by combining hard rock or heavy metal music with the Bugs gang.

That was a bit too radical for me, and, never the shy one, I said so. I'd been doing jingles and lyrics for Disney, and before that for clients like Kellogg's and Nestle. I was the expert. I settled in and put my feet on Greene's glass-top coffee table and expounded on my views.

"I think the Bugs' audience is pre-teens, the bubble-gum crowd," I said. "They go for their music a little more sugary."

"Yeah, maybe..." Steven eyed me over the lip of his styrofoam coffee cup, "but they look up to the older crowd."

I shrugged. My own hands were empty. Warner's Animation had the singularly worst coffee I'd ever tasted.

"I'm pretty sure Heavy Metal plays for an older audience," I said. "I'd bet the farm on it."

"Well, maybe you could knock it back a little." Steven was starting to get those little worry lines around the corners of his eyes, like maybe I didn't understand the depth of the excrement in which his show was bogged.

"*Restrained* Heavy Metal?" I scoffed.

"Hey," Greene said, giving up on me, "I don't want to tie your hands. Do what you think is best. The demographics say you did the job for Disney. Take your best shot for us."

We grappled a bit about money, and then I left for the Z's garage. The Z, alias The Cricket, alias Steve Zuckerman, is the world's greatest undiscovered musical genius. It's partly his own fault. Zuckerman's one of those guys who is easy to underestimate. He wears clothes you would have donated to the Salvation Army ten years ago, and he probably cuts his own hair, which he never combs, preferring the *apres la deluge* look.

But nobody hires the Z for his appearance. He's been working at his game for years, and he's a music maker the way I'm a film maker, that is, *he knows all the steps because he's done it all himself.* Very hard to pull the wool over his eyes. He's won about a zillion awards for his advertising music, and along the way he gradually transformed his garage into a wonderland of sound recording. I say he's undiscovered, because the big-time movie people are still snubbing him, passing him by for the kings of the kickback, and he's still waiting for his big break on the silver screen. Not that Z hasn't scored a movie or two. He did <u>Spawn of the Slithis</u>, a horror movie that was so bad, the only nice thing <u>Variety</u> said in the review was, "Excellent ominous musical provided by the very capable Steve Zuckerman."

Ideas come easily to me on the road, and so I write on scraps of paper while I'm driving. It seems to work okay; my writing is barely legible and so far I haven't hit anybody. Anyway, I'd had an idea in Greene's office, and, since the Z lived about 20 minutes away from the Warner's lot, I had most of the lyrics down by the time I got there.

I smacked the lyrics a second time, and Z spent a few hours hammering out a demo, flavor of the Beach Boys, and it went like this:

> It's cartoon gold/for young and old
> It's the Bugs Bunny/Road Runner Show
> The Bugs is hot/the Coyote's not
> And Road Runner's go-go-go
> (And they go)
> Beep-Beep-Beep-Beep
> Oom-Bapa-Mao-Mao
> Bubba-Bubba-Bub-a Bugs!

We followed with an instrument-only bed where we intro'ed the characters, and then did a repeat of the opening and we were out at 57 seconds, perfect for the show. The thing about Z that's really great, his demos are as good as most composers' finished products. I took the tape and slapped some visuals against the beat, just a rough storyboard but enough to pitch, and we went back out to Warner Bros. with the Z wearing a faded green velveteen shirt he must have stolen from a Navajo, a pair of rumpled mailman's trousers and some dusty go-aheads.

Greene didn't bat an eye at the Z's fashion statement, being used to creative types. He was moderately enthusiastic about the Beep-Beep song, which we had dubbed "It's Cartoon Gold" for obvious reasons. In fact, he popped for the cost to put the piece into production, which meant we would make a little money off the project, and for a few weeks life was happiness.

Now another thing that's really great about the Z is that he has spies everywhere. And so I wasn't surprised when he got back to me that Steven Greene had somebody else doing another demo. Not that Warner Brothers didn't have the right to do that. But my heart sank when I found out that this other guy was doing something cool, cutting-edge and *new wave*. Once again, I was competing against my boss.

"Probably won't even test 'em," I grumbled. "He's just going to pick his own favorite and children the world over will be deprived of our great song." That's me, at my surly worst. And I was dead wrong. He took both spots, the Beach Boys Beep-Beep and his own Super-cool number, and tested the hell out of them with all age groups of kids. The first hint we had that things were going our way, the Z's spies reported Greene was very unhappy with the results, and so he was taking both spots out and testing them again. And again. And every time, we won by a landslide. Beep-Beep-Beep-Beep Oom-Bappa-Mao-Mao. *The Z and I were gonna be on the air.*

162

Eyeballs & Eardrums

Every once in a while, somebody comes along who does a tremendous amount of good in the world. Seriously, now. Some of these people become legends, like Christ and Buddha. But a lot of them just go on spinning their good deeds, and not caring if they get recognized or not.

My friend Jim Hullihan is like that. He'd shrug and laugh it off if you called him a *buddhisatva*, or even a guy who is making a difference in the world. I call him *friend*, even though I haven't seen him in ten years. Actually, not since the great Eyeballs & Eardrums debacle. I'm not avoiding him. It's just that it's been painful thinking about what might have been.

Jim runs a nonprofit organization that creates multimedia shows for the purpose of motivating teenagers. There's no way of calculating how many lives he's touched in a positive way--hundreds of thousands, at the least. He would create one big show a year, and then his teams would fan out across the country to set up in high school gyms and theaters for what are called "assemblies". Each show of Jim's would have a theme, based on human values like courage, perseverance or patience. The way I'm describing it, the subject matter may seem dull, preachy and out of step

with the times; but once Jim finished with it, you would
never say that.

He went to all the top rock groups and got
permission to use their music, and even tapes of their
live performances and their rock videos. He begged
permission to use action clips of professional football,
basketball, baseball and ice hockey. He made the
rounds of all the major studios and picked short
segments of upcoming films. Finally, he shot thousands
of slides of high school kids in all their moods and habits,
and then skillfully mixed all these elements to where the
rock and movie stars and athletes all were in sync with
his theme.

The first time I met him, he called out of the blue,
one day in the early 80's, and invited me to come and
see his latest show. His pitch was that, if we would give
him some clips from our new movies, we would get the
free publicity that would come from tens of thousands of
moviegoing kids seeing them--and we'd be associated
with something worthwhile, to boot.

Well, sure, but it would be a cold day in hell, us
being a big studio and all...but I went to see his show,
which was all about the three "A's"--Attitude, Ability and
Adaptability. And I came away convinced.

I was impressed enough to push my waffle-y boss
in the right direction and we ended up giving Jim some
footage from Condorman, for his next year's theme,
which was going to be about role models. Condorman,
you may recall, was a live action story starring Michael
Crawford (in the paler days before he scored with
Phantom of the Opera). Michael plays a cartoon artist
who insists on dressing up and acting out the part of his
superheroes before he drew them.

I was really impressed by Jim's show. It was seen
by over 30% of the kids attending public schools in the
United States. His numbers were steadily rising, but he
was limited by the logistics--to put on the show, he

needed dependable teams who were willing to be on the road much of the year. The pay wasn't that great, and someone was always leaving to get married, settle down or go on tour as the electrician or gaffer with a rock band.

Now when you're working as a flack in the entertainment world, there aren't too many chances to do an obvious good thing for humanity. I'd earned plenty of chits in hell for earlier work I'd done on booze and smokes, and I wasn't going to let this chance to balance the scales pass me by. To make a long story short, I started to think of ways to take Jim's combination of motivation and entertainment and turn it into a weekly half-hour, a Saturday morning television show. It made a lot of sense to me--the show would hang onto the teens who were leaving the animated slushies they had watched as preteens.

And we were blessed with the serendipity of a historical event--Disney's EPCOT Theme Park, which professed to be all about the furthering of mankind, was to open in Florida in a little over a year, with all the grand hoopla associated with its billion dollar price tag. EPCOT had originally been Walt's idea for an experimental community to develop mankind along the road to peace and prosperity. It had somehow mushroomed into a gigantic theme park with a "World Village" of pavilions from many countries, and a variety of presentations mixing science and entertainment in hopefully correct dosages. And I knew something very few outsiders did--the Florida people and the very heads of Disney themselves were looking for television shows they could produce from EPCOT.

"Wow!" I thought, "This is perfect!"

I pushed my boss onto the bandwagon, and Jim and I started to format a show. We called it Eyeballs & Eardrums, because it was going to assail every youthful sense with our own balance of big-time athletes, rock stars and current movie madness--all woven with a backbone of thematic motivational messages. Jim stripped some glorious pieces from past shows, and I added some footage from the Disney animation vaults-- animation cut to rock music. These were the first "D-TV's", Disney's answer to MTV style quick-cuts. I'd originally produced them with Frank Brandt, cutter Roy Brewer, and Disney Exec Bob King as a 15-minute theatrical short called Disco Mickey Mouse, which ran with The Black Hole in 1979.

Once Jim and I had the presentation ready, my boss got very fidgety, refusing to view it himself. Instead, he arranged for a screening in the big theater for Ron Miller, the president of Disney! I guess I should have recognized the warning signals, but at the time, I was ecstatic.

Ron did show up, with a small battalion of mid-level executives, and they stayed for almost the entire screening. He even seemed to be enjoying it...until, near the end, I noticed one of the Disney lawyers whispering in his ear. At first, Ron seemed annoyed. But the lawyer spoke urgently, even insistently, until Ron got up and left. Once Ron left, so did everybody else.

My boss shook his head, his sign that I was, once again, in the deep doo-doo. "You gotta come with me," he said.

"Who else besides Ron did you tell about this?" I asked.

"You gotta come *NOW*," he insisted.

"Who *ELSE?*" I shouted.

"Well, just maybe a couple of the guys..." he mumbled weakly.

"Great. Just a couple of the guys," I repeated, the wind out of my sails.

"Come *ON. WE GOTTA GO!!*" His eyes were wide like he'd seen the second coming of Walt.

"Okay...let's go." I waved over my shoulder to Jim. "Pick up the film, Hullihan. I'll see what this is about."

I'll always remember the walk across Goofy Way from the studio to the Animation Building. I must not have been walking fast enough--knowing me, I had probably slowed down and was starting to get on the look of sullen black fury for which I was somewhat notorious. My boss actually took my shirtsleeve like I was a little kid and jerked me along to hurry me up! I pulled my arm away, and looked at him like he was nuts. We stood there in the middle of the street, looking like two morons from *The Apple Dumpling Gang*.

"COME *ON!!*" he shouted, fear flecking his lips, "They're waiting!"

And so I reluctantly followed him across the street, up the stairs (He wasn't willing to wait for the slow elevator, and Walt's fast elevator was at the other end of the long corridor.), and into the office of one of Disney's top lawyers, where the two of them took turns screaming at me. Screaming. Real screaming, like you see the bad guys do in <u>Home Alone</u>, or the chimps in the zoo when you tease them with peanuts and then don't throw them. *Didn't I know that, by working with an outsider, I was jeopardizing the entire EPCOT project? Copyrights and patents were at stake. We, the Walt Disney Organization, were now wide open to millions--no, TENS of millions of dollars worth of lawsuits!*

I let them rave about it for a while. Finally, when I saw that they weren't going to stop in the foreseeable future, I sighed and got up out of my chair.

"What did you think of the show?" I said quietly to the lawyer. I ignored my boss. In situations like this, it's always best to work on them one at a time.

This lawyer was a little guy with a big mouth and a red-hot temper.

"Didn't you hear a word we said?!" he screamed. "Who gives a shit about the show?!"

"I do," I said, and I started out of his office.

My boss got up out of his chair to block me.

"Don't touch me," I said. "I've got a thing about it. It makes me a little crazy."

"You're making a big mistake," he said, but he backed away even as the words came out of his mouth.

"Maybe. But I'm just losing my temper. You guys are losing a great show." I flicked a thumb back at the lawyer, now turning my back to him and giving my boss the full attention, "How can you put up with this weasel shit?"

"Well...the studio has to be protected...", he said weakly.

"Bull. These guys just want to be producers. 'Little Hitlers, one and all', your exact words. 'They run around confusing Ron, who's already confused enough in his own mind', exact words you've also said."

I left the two of them looking uneasily at each other and went back to find Jim and make my apologies. In the next few days, the legal department fired me memo after memo, demanding Jim and I sign over all rights to the show to Disney. I ignored them as long as I could and finally drafted my own little memo saying that the two of us had no plans to take over EPCOT by devious legal means or actual guerilla warfare, and Jim and I signed that.

But the Eyeballs & Eardrums project was a dead fish. You know how that is. Nobody would touch it. A few months later, another Disney executive who was a bit better plugged into the system actually did a show for EPCOT. It featured a talking purple dragon and a frizzy-haired wizard of science. It cost millions of dollars to develop and in the end was so bad they never could run it anywhere. A terrible, terrible show. A total loss, all that money down the drain. I shook my head and went back to my old job, huckstering dog movies from Disney.

The D-TV format, of course, became very popular on the Disney Channel for a while, until they realized how the technique "burned the library", one two-and-a-half minute song needing the key footage from as many as five or six cartoons, if you were lucky. And, believe it or not, they promoted the guy who'd done that awful Frizzy-Wizard-and-Dragon business to Vice President and gave him a big raise.

Frogs Ain't Funny

Today animation gets enormous help from computer electronics, but there was a time a few decades ago when it wasn't so. In those Neanderthal Times, which stretched nearly into the mid-1980's, it was an odd and sad thing to see fine artists caught in the web of television cartoon animation, chained, as it were, to their animation stands, jailed in their tiny cubicles, which stretched on and away down the corridor like so many little prisons. Of course, there always was television animation, and then there was *classic* animation, and it was somewhat different if you were working on an animated feature. Then you could remember the consummate artistry of <u>Snow White and The Seven Dwarves</u>, the rich and colorful storytelling of <u>Pinocchio</u> and know there was a great light at the end of your long dark tunnel.

But if you were working on television animation, whether it was storyboarding, animating, or in-betweening, you were truly caught in the jaws of hell. There you were, with a firm wrist and the drawing skills of a young Michelangelo, animating frame after frame of a silly, slobbery dog, or a dopey, heroic duck, or even an anthropomorphic turtle. It was enough to cause the heroic figures on the ceiling of the Sistine Chapel to break down and weep.

The problem, simply stated, was not artistic so much as it was arithmetic. Motion picture film goes through a projector at a rate of 24 frames a second (25 in England). That's 1,440 frames a minute, or 28,800 frames in the 20 minutes of a brainless half hour kiddie show, the part that is not set aside for commercials. Think about it. Somebody of enormous talent and patience had to put aside his or her creativity to draw all that drivel.

In the ancient days when I worked at Hanna-Barbera, ancestral home of Saturday Morning television cartoon shows, I noticed a lot of deep despair and gallows humor coming from the ordinary, everyday art people. They talked much about being "wrists without brains", and about "drawing their lives away". There was a certain mixture of envy and pride when they retold the legend of Joe Ruby and Kenny Spears, two lowly film editors who studied Bill Hanna and Joe Barbera's sense of humor so well that they became writers, and eventually produced shows of their own. Ruby and Spears, as the story went, did a script chock-full of their bosses' hairiest gags and oldest pratfalls, and Bill and Joe thought it was the brightest, funniest, freshest script they'd ever seen that they themselves hadn't actually written.

While I was hearing all this grousing from the caged ones, I don't know that I was particularly empathetic to it. I think I felt it was only natural, considering the onerous nature of their discipline. I really didn't understand what it was all about. After all, they were *getting paid*, weren't they? They could always paint significant art on their own time (as so many of them did and still do). That was before my infamous Woodsy Owl presentation.

You know Woodsy Owl, Smokey the Bear's ecology-minded friend. Everybody does. Bill Hanna had invented him a few years before, and written some words to an old lullaby that they had donated to the National Forest Service. But the H&B folks didn't just fall off the turnip truck; if they could get a show out of this, they could draw a line in the sand of the Great Wasteland for the educational and environmental creeps who were howling that their Saturday Morning fare was "junk food for the mind".

Their problem was, Woodsy wasn't the normal pratfall or action-adventure kind of guy that Bill and Joe understood so well. He had to be a teacher figure, instilling values and learning as well as laughs and action.

So the word went out through the H&B empire that they were seeking enlightenment and would be open to ideas on how to make Woodsy fly. I was still young enough to go ecstatic over that kind of invite. I knew most of the animators, had joshed around in their dark cells, and so I went looking for a partner with a wrist. You see, nobody in animation, which is a visual medium, thinks much of an idea from a writer. If it's not drawn on paper, they can't see how it's going to work out, they have trouble *visualizing* it.

My search for an artist partner took about a week, and in the end crashed unsuccessfully with a dull thud. Wherever I went, I was met with incredulous jeers and sardonic whoops. *Bill and Joe are gonna let you do what?! You're actually gonna be able to think up your own characters?! Your own story sits? Naaaaa. Get out of here, kid, before I make you into hamburger.*

For my part, I wasn't very charitable. *They were all hopeless fools, so deep in their own misery they couldn't see the life raft when somebody tossed it to them!* I wouldn't give up, and finally, in one of the deepest, lowest cells situated furthest away from Bill and Joe's offices, I found one last artist who seemed to have a little spark left. He was a young Japanese guy. He grinned at me and said the journey was everything, he would do it for the experience. His eyes twinkled as he accepted, and I had the uneasy feeling that he was laughing at me.

We got down to the hard business of professional creating, that is, creating something on time, on target and on budget. In our sessions we hammered out our characters, fleshing their personalities and characteristics. The assignment really wasn't that hard; it boiled down to finding a few sidekicks for Woodsy. The story, like all Saturday Morning television, would be the same one, over and over, with minor variations-- Woodsy and his pals would thwart an odd assortment of polluters, greedy businessmen and thoughtless human "guests of the forest", who were about to destroy it. Smokey couldn't appear, even as a guest shot, so I guessed there was some question of rights there; I never asked.

My Japanese partner and I came up with a wonderful trio--Woodsy Owl, a Cougar named Ed, and a Frog we called Freddy Flip-Flop. I'd always had a thing for the deep-voiced Froggie on the old Buster Brown radio show, so I thought a flap-lipped hopper of a buddy was a good counterpoint to Woodsy, who would be our brainy, if absentminded professor, and Ed Cougar, a somewhat dim fellow who would supply the muscle to get the other two out of jams.

My partner did boards on the characters, showing views of what they looked like alone and together. I took an old story bible from The Flintstones and used the format to produce one for our new Woodsy show. Verily, plain to see, we had our excrement together.

However, Joe made it clear from the start he didn't want to see the presentation. He didn't want anything to do with it. His excuse was, he said it was Bill's gig. So we gained an audience and marched into Bill's office. It didn't have the feel of a happy meeting from the very start. Bill seemed disturbed by the extent of the work we'd done. "You didn't have to go to all this kind of *detail*," he said weakly, "after all, I'm *in the business*. I can *see* an idea."

But we had done all that we had done, and I was adamantine about presenting it. Bill sighed and settled in for the duration. I had the mental image he was putting on a set of heavy-duty earmuffs, but I couldn't figure out why. About halfway through I saw he was fighting us so hard he was unconsciously shaking his head at the points as we made them. We continued, and so did he, tiny little shakes from side to side.

After the longest half-hour I could remember, we finally finished. There was a long pause, and then Bill said, "Thank you. You boys have done quite a bit of work..." Here he eyed me, "But you should have talked to me first."

"Why, Bill?" I asked, getting that old sinking feeling in the pit of my stomach.

"I could have straightened you out right away about some of the things that don't work."

"What things?"

"Just about everything. It's impossible. We just can't do it."

"But for *what reason?*" I cried, desperate for an answer even as I saw that there never would be one. Not a real answer. He didn't have one. In his own way, Bill was just as desperate as we were. He blathered about this and that, reaching for something, anything, and he finally said, "And most of all, we can't do a frog. Now *dogs* are funny. And some birds, though you always have the stiff-beak problem. Even your cougar could be a little funny. But frogs just aren't funny."

I suppose it wasn't clever to argue further with the king of TV animation, who was known to be a touch bristly and short-tempered, but I'd never been known as a fount of wisdom. My voice rose to a challenge, "I don't see how you can say that!"

Bill eyed me coldly, giving me that *and who the hell are you, kid* look, "We've never done a frog here at H-B.

And in all these years, Warners and U.A. have never done a frog. Friz Freleng never did a frog. Walter Lantz never did a frog. For God's sake, *Disney himself* never did a frog! Don't you think there was a reason, Jack?! All these great men of animation, and here you are, coming in here and trying to tell me frogs are funny!"

It was a crazy, unexpected line of logic, and I didn't really know how to talk my way out of it. I halfheartedly mentioned Mr.Toad, but Bill dismissed him with a mild, deprecatory raspberry of the lips. And that was it. My partner and I snatched our presentation and retreated in a semi-panic before the fury of one of the leading men of animation. Our defeat was so complete and final that we never did regroup. My partner went back to his dark cell at the far end of the animation building, Freddy Flip-Flop died the death, and we left the solution of the Woodsy show to other, wiser heads.

Bill was a giant creator, and he had built a huge empire based on his and Joe's ideas. He knew that once accepted, every idea needed thousands and thousands of hours of manpower to bring it to the television screen. He just wasn't comfortable working with my young partner and me. We should have tried to find some middle ground the way Ruby and Spears had. We should have run some old Tom & Jerry shows before we started. Maybe we should have boned up on our Flintstone gags. Maybe if the frog had been a hound, or had talked like Barney Rubble...

We had come up with some fresh and new ideas, but they were quite a bit different from your ordinary Bill-and-Joe fare. Bill instinctively didn't like them, but he honestly couldn't tell us why. And when the chips were down, the only way he could explain it was to attack the freshest, funniest part of our presentation.

Frogs are not now, never were, and never will be funny. You can quote Bill Hanna on that. That was a long time ago, and by now I'm more or less resigned to it. I'm just glad nobody ever told Jim Henson or Kermit.

The Loneliness of the Long-Distance Runner

One of the things you learn when directing stars is that, while they do what they do very well, they only do it within a certain range that is uniquely specific to their genius. For instance, cowpoke Dennis Weaver was marvelous as long as you never asked him to deliver more than 20 or so words in a half-minute. Try to get him to rush it to get in another copy point and Dennis starts to sound like the whiney Festus, his role on the old Gunsmoke television show. John Wayne was the same way. Try rushing, "What are you tryin' to say, Pilgrim?" Orson Welles was the same way--there was a guy who simply could never find a second way to say anything. He was Orson, he was the original, and if it didn't sound right to you, you'd better write a different line.

I was in charge of such things when Orson did a half-hour radio show for Disney, a narrated radio version of Ray Bradbury's original <u>Something Wicked This Way Comes</u>, and believe me, nobody really directs Orson Welles. You just sit back and let it roll, and if you want another take, you, you cut in and say there was a mechanical error or the soundman forgot to punch *record* at the right moment, and would he please be so kind as to do another take?

Professional voice talent is the same way. Voice narrator Danny Dark has a great, marvelously distinctive voice, but he only does it one way, the distinctive Danny Dark way, and you love him for it. Percy Rodriguez has a deep voice-of-God delivery, but you don't ask God to pick up his pace, you cut the copy. Robert Conrad is the same way. I once requested he hurry some lines for a trailer promoting <u>The Last Flight of Noah's Ark</u>. I'd shelled out $50,000 for an hour of his time, and the copy was such a bad fit that the CEO of Disney Studios demanded angrily, "Who is that silly tub-thumper?"

A second thing is that, while certain stars need to build through several takes to their best performance, with some actors the first take is all you get. Frank Sinatra was a notorious one-take guy. I directed lots of Leslie Nielsen commercials for Ford Corporate, and, although Leslie would give you as many takes as you wanted, his first or second readings were usually his best. After that, he seemed to flatten out and lose interest. Of course, the subtext in commercials is simply "buy this product", so maybe you can't blame him.

Beyond that, when you get away from stars and begin to direct personalities, new cans of worms, worms beyond belief, will appear out of nowhere. I've never directed Tony Hillerman, the great writer of Navajo detective novels, but I've heard him speak and doubt I could ever do much that might be helpful. Tony sparkles on the written page. Tony in person will put you to sleep. On the other end of the spectrum, George Plimpton was as polished a speaker as any actor, and working with him was pleasant and even wonderful. In the middle of this broad range you find personalities, people with great talent that is tantalizingly just out of reach, talent that begs for a great director to bring it to light. Alas, I said a *great* director, to which I might add *enough time and budget to make the magic happen.*

Once, I had to direct famous long-distance runner Billy Mills to do the voice-over narration for a documentary on his life. It was a half hour show I produced at Disney to go along with the motion picture Running Brave.

Billy was an Oglala Sioux, born on the reservation near Pine Ridge, South Dakota in 1938. His story was that, as a young Native American Indian, he had been a natural born runner. As a kid he loved to run wild and free with the wind in his hair. But when he went to the University of Kansas in the late 1950's, he had to tame his skills and run on command. This was a different skill, something alien to the Native American Indian way of thinking. As the story in the movie goes, Billy finally finds a college coach who understands him, and he learns to compete in an arena that, in more innocent times, we might have called *the white man's world.* His real-life story was naturally more complex, but basic beats were about the same and, overall, it certainly was a dramatic life. After college he joined the U.S. Marines. They allowed him to train as a runner, and in 1964 he qualified to run on the U.S. team in the 10,000-meter race in the Tokyo Olympics.

Well, in that year, English miler Ron Clarke was the huge favorite, followed by the talented Tunisian runner Mohamed Gammoudi. No American had ever won the 10,000, and the handicappers gave Billy no chance at all. As the race progressed, Mills was pushed behind the front runners by the superior tactics of Clarke and Gammoudi. The leaders were setting a fast pace, and by the last lap, though Mills was close he was not close enough. In fact, he was stuck behind the leaders who had effectively walled him off. He made a desperate move on the backstretch, going around the outside, but they held firm and he couldn't move in front. In fact, footage shows that Billy was shoved out of his lane. Now he was clearly exhausted, and the broadcaster commenting on the race entirely forgot about him. As they approached the final turn, Billy did something totally outrageous and seemingly foolish--he ran outside the other two runners, a tactic that meant he had to run much faster just to keep up. Again he got a push for his efforts, but the one thing it did for him was to give him a clear outside position coming out of the turn, a position that the two other men couldn't block without fouling him.

What happened next was the stuff of legends, one of the golden moments in sports history, a finish that stunned spectators and provided one of the greatest upsets in Olympic history. You can hear it today and it is guaranteed to give you the shivers--the runners are just coming out of the turn when the broadcaster wakes up and realizes what's happening. He's intoning, "Yes, yes, it looks like Clarke...now Gammoudi is trying but to no avail...yes...no, it's Clarke...and--AND, MY GOD, HERE COMES--IT'S...IT'S BILLY MILLS! Billy Mills is coming up on the outside. Billy Mills is moving. Billy Mills is dead even. Billy Mills is moving ahead!"

Well, that was the fabulous history. Billy the-man-the-myth-the-person himself showed up at Disney Studios in Burbank the afternoon before our recording session. He had to do the normal PR things and so I didn't have much time to get to know him, which in director's language means I had no time to get him to like me, trust me, or even understand me. A director has to be able to convey those sort of links with talent. Ordinarily, with professional voice talent, that's not a problem. They know what they can do; in fact, they've been hired to do just what they do best. Being a professional with some experience, I also know what to expect, and we go through the sessions mostly just smoothing out the little bumps for the studio and advertising execs, who naturally have their own fears and bosses to report to.

I didn't know what to expect. The truth is, you never do know how people who don't do it for a living are going to act when they get behind a mike, and I like to be prepared. Billy did drop by. In our initial meeting at my office (at that time I had an office on the lot in the Roy O. Disney building, prestigious with windows and everything) I was tremendously impressed with him. He had a soft, warm voice and a warm and personable manner. At that time he was probably in his mid-50s, and a famous ex-athlete who had become a hugely successful promotional speaker. Hey, the guy was used to speaking, this was going to be a piece of cake! I don't know why, just some sixth sense prompted me to ask him to read a few lines from the script I'd written. What a difference! There was this sudden weird shift in our relationship. His entire presence shifted to one of stony separation. Billy Mills may have been a great public speaker, but it didn't look like he could read lines of narration from a page. We went over it again. And again. It didn't get better, it got worse. His delivery was that of a stone man. He read as if he'd been eating Dairy Queens until his brain and lips were both frozen stiff.

I could see I was going to have an enormous problem with Billy. The real Hollywood moves fast and it never looks back. That meant I was only going to get one shot. I figured it was my problem, and it was probably me, the director, at fault. Billy didn't know me. I figured he thought I was the establishment, the hotshot Disney director. He had to get to know me. Once he saw I was just an ordinary fellow, same as anybody else in his audience, he could unfreeze and go back to being his warm and wonderful self.

I was trying to set him at ease, to let him know I was just an ordinary guy. I mentioned I had a blood brother who was a Navajo. That earned me a cold look. I could see my comment was a little like telling a Frenchman you knew somebody who was Greek. I was really behind the curve on this one.

Now, at that time, I was staying in pretty good shape. I ran daily and did 10 K races a few times a year. I wasn't very fast or good, but I didn't pretend to be. In my own humble way, I too liked the wind in my hair, the racer's high they call it. So the thought came to me that we could run together. I suggested we meet the following morning outside his hotel and jog so we could talk over his lines as we went. Well, I didn't sell that idea very well; Billy looked at me as he'd probably looked at thousands of wanna-be runners over the years who would have liked to tell their beer buddies they whupped the great Billy Mills in a foot race.

"I don't think so," he said.

I felt my face going beet red.

"See you at the recording session," I said. "Tomorrow. Two o'clock sharp."

I don't ordinarily give up so easily, but I felt like crawling under the nearest pile of scripts and never coming out. Me, who went out of his way never to stare or shake hands or cop a star autograph, accused of chumming up to greatness.

The next day, Billy did the session, and in spite of every trick I knew, he was awful. I absolutely couldn't get him out of his shell. I tried friendly. I tried tricky and cunning. I tried professionally aloof. And, as a last resort, I tried the only thing left--I bullied him. Oddly enough, this worked, though only to the degree that, instead of pathetic, his reading assumed something of a quietly controlled professionalism.

So you see, I never actually solved the problem, and it annoys me to this day that I couldn't figure out how to do it. Somewhere inside Billy Mills is a warm and wonderful storyteller, the guy he was in that first moment when the PR folks handed him off to me. But I never was able to persuade that inner person to come out and narrate the film that, ironically, was about his greatest deeds. That left me to realize that people who aim high and are in it for the long haul aren't going to win every race. You do your best with what you've got, and if you win the Oscar or the Emmy you take it home. And if you don't, you grit your teeth a little and then you suck it up and go on to the next script, the next pitch, the next project. Because the serious talents in the games we play here in Hollywood are all long-distance runners.

One Good Client Is Worth a Thousand Words

As a journeyman (journey*person*) copywriter, you can toil away in the gloom for what seems like a millennium, looking for the light, spilling out page after page of marvelous, on-target copy--and still be ashamed to tell the gang at your class reunion what you do for a living. Sometimes it seems like creating ads is two different games. There's the common ritual of doing boring, on-target stuff that keeps a check coming your way every two weeks. And then there are the breakthrough assignments, the treasured work where everything just flows, your ideas flutter, dip and curve and your verbs sink just right into the strike zone. To use my father's old South Chicago expression, *How come is that?*

Well, for one thing, you say, it's the nature of the product. If you're doing lag-lines for a new Clive Barker horror flick, your creative juices are naturally stimulated. *Bowling for Blood*, you write. *Your skin crawls...right off your body*, you write. The ideas swarm around your head like pesky vampire bats. Writing for something interesting like a movie is surely easier and more fun than trying to get response out of tire dealers for a high-grade polyurethane tire fill, you say. But think again; that's not necessarily so.

I remember when I was at Disney trying to come up with a campaign for director Carroll Ballard's quasi-epic nature film <u>Never Cry Wolf</u>. Even though Farley Mowat's famous novel was crystal-clear storytelling, Carroll had been trying to figure out what his movie adaptation was about for most of the several years he was taking to shoot it, and the budget had tripled in the interim. His contract said he had to turn in the picture "within six months after completion of principal photography", so every time the deadline got close, *Mister Name-Above-The-Title* ducked north and cranked off some more footage. Hey, maybe you would too, if you had 200,000 feet in the can of a guy and a wolf looking at each other and no reason why. They had wolf-actors that grew old and died on that picture. Big problem. Worse yet, Carroll was one of these film guys who wanted to be "intimately involved" in the marketing of his epic, and yet trying to work out a viable concept with him was like smoking ganja with a guru; he would talk forever, getting off on ethereal stuff about nature, the Eskimos, God, man and the animals until you wanted to knot his director's viewfinder around his neck and ship him back to the arctic rim. Maybe you saw him on the talk shows after the film was finished and out in theaters. He was still waving his arms around, voicing vague mumbo about man's foolish inhumanity and the sanctity of the animals. This from the guy who had the animal rights activists swarming his tail for alleged horse cruelties when he was making <u>The Black Stallion</u>. No wonder the marketing creative players in the entertainment biz burn out like Christmas tree bulbs.

On the other hand, once when I was freelancing, I ran across a bright client named Ransome Wyman. A self-made chemist/inventor and businessman, Ransome was the son of a bible-belting minister, and he himself had seen the light--that is, he believed in the power of advertising that interested and excited people.

Ransome's company sold a dull and boring product with the added problem that it was invisible--it was a soft polyurethane tire fill called RePneu that replaced the air in off-road vehicles like garbage trucks, mining and factory vehicles and road graders so they never went flat. You may never have heard of it, but polyurethane tire fill has the potential to be a fairly universal product; a road grader with a blown tire, for instance, can cost a construction company thousands of dollars a day while the workers sit around waiting for a replacement. Problem was, back then most tire dealers treated the tire refill industry like the plague. Their attitude was, *Who wants something that makes tires last forever?!*

Ransome's solution was to hire the brightest writer he could find (me) to produce a quarterly newsletter for dealer distribution. We hammered away at product quality, low cost of installation machinery, and particularly at the extra money that dealers could make as "tire fill" guys. And we did more than that. We created a selling atmosphere. We invented an irreverent "No Bull" money-back guarantee and designed a chatty, even witty style for the paper. We called it REPNEUS and gave it the waggish flagline *All the pneus that's phit to print.* There were articles about product development, rebate ads for the slow months, human interest stories, quotes and wise sayings, a comic strip and a one-panel cartoon, all relating to the industry. We even went historical with a tongue-in-cheek column called Rubber is Interesting Stuff, explaining how Columbus found the native Americans bouncing rubber balls, how Clark Gable went west to Hollywood from a job in the Firestone plant in Akron, and how Hitler might have won the war had he used tire fill (no flats to slow down his *blitzkrieg).* Good, on-target stuff, and generally fun to write.

Well, as for the Never Cry Wolf situation, I eventually gave up and hired out to NY ad mavens Canut, Manager & Deutsch for some low-concept high-price commercials. (Lots of times the powers-that-be will buy the approach if it comes from a name boutique and costs enough.) "Okay," the wise men of C, M & D said, gazing idly from their penthouse windows at the staggering view of the urban canyons below, "But we're busy guys. We'll fit it in, as long as we don't have to deal with Carroll..."

I have no complaints. It was no blockbuster, but they did a decent job for <u>Never Cry Wolf</u>. On the other hand, after two years, the bright little <u>REPNEUS</u> newsletter had increased the entire tire-fill market by 15% and raised Ransome's share-of-market from 45 to 55%. Ransome knew what his product needed, he knew how to articulate what he wanted, and I had fun working with him. That's a good client. And a good client is worth a thousand words. Which is what this is, more or less.

On Being Accepted by the Client

Once when I was freelance writing, I got a call from a harried young Creative Director who worked for a small, design-oriented ad agency on Beverly over near Fairfax in the Mid-Wilshire section of Los Angeles. This time he was more agitated than usual, and so I got him to stop hyperventilating and to bare his soul even before the mandatory fee discussion. Freelancers tend to be a hard-bitten bunch, but the tale he told was enough to make a grown man weep. Apparently, they were having enormous copy problems with a super-high quality metal alloys company. This company made metals which were used to create sophisticated machines which in turn were used to manufacture things that went very fast under difficult circumstances, like the B-2 bomber and the Stealth Fighter. My friend's ad agency had been hired to produce a glossy brochure touting their capabilities. But the problem wasn't the know-how needed to pen such a brochure--it was a client out of control to the point of rabidity. They were actually afraid he was going to bite somebody.

My friend begged poverty and I skeptically agreed to a few thousand dollars, with my famous revisions escape clause (I recommend it to all freelancers) that would pay me $50 an hour after I turned in the first draft plus one brush-up. And then I showed up the next day at the metal alloys company, cursing myself because it was way across town and I hadn't thought to charge for drive time.

I was five minutes early; but when I walked in they'd already started the bloodletting. You could hear the screaming from the reception area. The receptionist, an innocent young thing with purple eyelids and pink dagger fingernails, apologized and led me into the beating room where the company prez was taking his turn at the plate. It didn't take much to see it was always his turn. My poor friend, the CD, was looking wildly around for an escape hatch or a rope ladder while the prez waved a batch of papers in the air and yelled, "This is beetle dung! You wrote this copy yourself, didn't you, you little twerp?! And you have the nerve to show up here in person!"

It was a problem you run across a lot as a freelancer, particularly when you work for the smaller agencies. This CD had come from the art direction side of the business, but, having passed high school English, he'd convinced himself and a considerable group of other people who should have known better that he was a writer. Sometimes you can get away with it for years, the common perception in these circles being that *everybody's* a writer. But now real life had reared its ugly head, the subjects and predicates refused to lay right in their little lines on the page, and his client had him in full retreat. The prez was actually banging his fists on the table like a chimp, just like they do in those bad movies about advertising written by people who have never been in the business.

The CD, overjoyed for the interruption caused by my entrance, leapt to his feet to make the introductions. I shook hands with the prez, his wife the treasurer, his son the flunky gofer, and his weather-beaten chief engineer. There was a brief two seconds of silence while we all looked at each other, and then the prez started in again, only now he was yelling *at me.*

"Blinding incompetence! I find it everywhere! There is no service left in America! Nobody cares! Nobody strives to excel! I don't have to put up with it! I could write this stuff myself!" After each short sentence, he banged the table with his fists. It was quite a show. I figured right away the money wasn't going to be worth it.

"You probably could," I replied agreeably. "Why don't you?"

The young CD's mouth dropped open. This wasn't exactly what he'd signed me on for. His tortured look spelled *traitor*. His hands fluttered to his twisted mouth, which was trying to say *Shhhhhh*, *Nooooooo* and *Ohhhh God* at the same time.

The prez went on yelling at me as if I hadn't spoken a word. If anything, he tweaked his volume up a notch. "I tell you, *it isn't that difficult!* It's just English, for cryin' out loud! I *do* know the *language!*" He shook the wilting pages in his hand, "I could write this!!"

"Yes," I said, still quiet, but a little more firmly, "Why don't you?"

By now the CD was ready to jump out the window, which might have been dramatic but would only have gotten him dusty as we were on the first floor. I noticed with some interest that his face had the patchy white-and-red blotched look that precedes a heart attack.

The prez, still talking as if he hadn't heard me, roared in my face, "I *said, I could write this!!!*" With that, he shredded the old copy and threw it in the air.

"I heard you. Who could not? The deaf, the dead heard you. And *I* said, 'Why don't you?' You're obviously the best man for the job."

He sat down, actually seeing me for the first time. The wind visibly went out of him, like his chest was one of those balloons when you let go of the end. "Because," he said, "I don't want to. That's what we hired you for."

"Well then," I said, "let's get to it."

The rest of the meeting was complicated, high-tech wise, but reasonably amicable. After an hour, I stood and put away my notes, feeling I had everything I needed to pull off a first draft. As I got to the door, the prez's sardonic voice overtook me, "So, when do we see you again? Two weeks? This project's later than a ten-month baby now!"

"Tomorrow morning at 8. That soon enough?"

He grumbled as to how it was.

I had to work most of the night, and showed up on the doorstep of the metal alloys company the next morning in a foul humor. Mil Spec writing does that to you; it's the perfect combination of technical jargon, military double-speak and sales babble, enough to make you lose your mind. It requires a special mood, like writing about superior bedpans or bank certificates of deposit, and I usually try to avoid the blank page for two or three days before taking the plunge.

The prez was alone in the big conference room, waiting for me, when I walked in. He glanced at his watch, but there was no satisfaction there. It was 8 on the dot. I laid the first draft, about 20 pages of work, in front of him with the majesty of an old monk presenting his hand-lettered life's work to the abbot. He read the first line and glanced up at me, shaking his head, "We don't usually use this tone of voice--" He pointed down to the page, inviting me to take a look.

I waved him off with a negligent toss of my hand, "I don't write it a sentence at a time, and I don't expect you to read it that way. Do me the professional courtesy to read it through, and then we'll talk."

He gave me a brief grunt and went back to his reading. After making his way through the first page, he mumbled, "I see where it's going now. Nice touch. I like it."

He finished his first read and called in his wife and kid and the engineer. He was in the middle of praising me for the great professional writer I really am when he felt a sudden call of nature. As the private bathroom was right next to the conference room, he left the door open and continued talking while he unzipped and started to relieve himself. I basked in the warm glow of his praise, looking at the dusty, sunlit trees in the parking lot and listening to the melodious rise and fall of his voice over the tinkle in the toilet. I was a member of the family.

Goofy Over the Falls

Sound effects people have a language all their own. Some of their words and the effects they stand for are common to sound departments in every studio around town ("Walla", or "Crowd Walla", for instance, which means a particularly bland background crowd noise). Others are peculiar and even trademarked to a particular studio. The slide whistle drop of Wile E. Coyote from a cliff can be found at Warner Bros. Animation, on the shelf near the Road Runner's "Beep Beep". An EFX reel labeled "Yabba Doo's", and the slappy sound of Fred running followed by a whistle of wind, could only come from the basement of Hanna-Barbera, and both would be properly filed under <u>The Flintstones</u>.

Sound effects cutters, or EFX cutters, as they are known, tend to be sharing and considerate fellows. When one or the other of them is faced with a problem, say to create the sound of tropical rain on a thousand barrels of cocaine waiting to be shipped out of the Columbian jungles, or of a cartoon nose being stretched like a rubber banana, if the solution is not at hand, they will quite likely spread their problem to the community. And, like as not, somebody from Universal will send over a cavalry charge which, when speeded up just right sounds like rain on a thousand barrels. And a fellow deep in the bowels of Paramount will pick up the phone and play a tape of a Booooing! noise that maybe/maybe-not works for the nose.

Now Disney of all the studios has always been considered the pioneer of sound effects. Some historians will tell you that Disney's 8th dwarf, the merry, rotund Jimmy MacDonald, practically invented the craft, or at least elevated it to the disciplines of a profession. Some of the machines he created for Snow White, the world's first full-length animated feature, would have made Rube Goldberg drool with envy. He built his strange and amazing devices out of the hubris of our mechanical society, out of marbles, washtubs, and sewing machine trundles, from whucka-board and cellophane and ball bearings and a thousand other things. But Jimmy's inventions worked so well--sounded so right--that many are still in demand today. And the Disney sound department, like all the others in Hollywood, makes them and the noises they create available to the rest of the studios as a professional courtesy. That is, all except for the sound effect known as "Goofy Over The Falls".

In one sense, you can argue that "Goofy Over The Falls" isn't really a sound effect at all, in that it's the famous utterance that slaphappy Disney dog-person first made as he headed over a waterfall. Goofy opens his mouth and yells something like, *"Ya Ahh-ha-ha-hoooooooooiiiiieeee!"* It's an almost indescribable sound, but one that, once you've heard it, you'll never forget.

It was probably first recorded in the late 30's or early 40's, and it was later used in other shows starring the Goof, among them "Goofy Goes Skiing" and "Lion Around" (when the Goof stumbles off his high-rise penthouse and begins the world's longest animated free fall). It's the sound a cartoon character makes, as specific and identifiable to Goofy as, say, the quacky duck voice is to Donald, or the high-register mousey voice is to Mickey. But, while Goofy's normal guffaw and his outrageous chuckle are easy to imitate, this one "Goofy Over The Falls" was unique. It had a rare, echo-ey timbre, it resonated with a certain joy-in-the-face-of-absolute-disaster that had to come from the very soul of the funny bone of the guy, unnamed and lost to history, who originally vented it.

Whenever it was used, it was heavily mixed with gurgling water or rushing wind or music, so it couldn't be "swiped clean" and used for something else. And it was never, ever to be let out of the studio.

By the end of the 80's, long after I'd left Disney and was producing shows through my own Happyfeets Company, "Goofy Over The Falls" was still the exclusive province of The Mouse Factory (as the lot is known to those of us who've done time there). I was producing Here Comes Sam, a special for the Disney Channel. I'd written and produced a snappy little half hour telling how the studio had come up with the idea for creating "Sam, the Olympic Eagle", the mascot for the 1984 L.A. Olympics. Pumped by how well the special worked, the channel execs asked me to expand it to an hour show. Time was short, but I'd written lyrics for a few D-TVs (M-TV style clips using Disney animated footage), and I figured, with a trip to Florida to capture Sam dancing at the newly opened EPCOT theme park, we'd be home free.

But I'd miscalculated. There's no commercial fill in a cable hour--at least, there wasn't any back then. When you did a network show, it was 47 minutes of programming, more or less. But my cable show had to be 57:56, nearly a full hour of entertainment. I'd plumped out the show, racking my brain for every idea and scrap of footage remotely related to the creation of Sam, but I was starting to run a little lean and the show was still *major short*, as the writers say. Where was I going to get that last ten minutes? I put in another stanza of cute little Sam dancing to the title song and chroma-keyed slides of Americana behind him. I did some more interviews with Disney artists and craftsmen, even with some of the disgruntled losers who thought the Olympic mascot should have been a frog, a rattlesnake, a beaver or a sea lion. Even with these editions, it was going to be very close.

It all came down to a late night edit session at Vidtronics, the tape editing house where Disney kept videotape masters of their cartoons in a big vault. I had written one last song, "Olympic Goof" (He's one-hundred proof! Oooooooooo-lympic Goof!). The tape editor and I cut down an old (Disney prefers the word *classic)* 15 minute cartoon "Goofy Track & Field" to fit the song, which ran two minutes and 40 seconds, just enough to give us what we needed. I had the show to length. There was only one spot in the song that could use a little help. It was where Goofy pole-vaults high into the sky over the Coliseum. He hesitates for a moment, holds his nose, and then begins his plummet back to the turf. Usually, if we were cutting on film, the sound EFX guys would slap something wild on another reel and send it over to the studio theater, where the studio mixers would sync it on the fly and mix it in. But we were in a Videotape edit bay miles from the studio. It was the middle of the night, and the sound department was surely all home a-snug in their beds.

That's when I remembered "Lion Around" had a "Goofy Over The Falls" in it. I remembered it as being fairly clean. My editor, Jerry, sent a runner down to the vaults to dig it out. We got the reel and he slapped in the effect in no time. It worked perfectly, Goofy's crazy call coming just as the force of gravity took over and rocketed him dizzily back to earth.

I knew how protective the Disney sound guys were about this one particular EFX, but there really wasn't going to be any problem; the Goof's wild *Yaahh-ha-ha-ha-hoooooooiiiiieee!* wasn't in the clear, it was protected by the hard driving sound of "Olympic Goof", the music we'd mixed in with it.

We put the show to bed and finished the session at
3:30 in the morning. The last thing we did was clean up
the bay and stack our source tapes on a cart so the
runner could take them back to the vault. Jerry and I
walked to the parking lot together. He crawled into his
Alfa sportster and buzzed out of the lot, heading up Vine
Street toward the Cahuenga pass. Too tired to think, I
watched him go for a minute and then piled in my old
BMW and started the 20 mile drive home to Woodland
Hills, hands gripping the wheel and eyes blinking wide in
the state of awareness reserved for the living dead and
for those who do 18 hour nonstop edit sessions.

And within a week, the clean version of the last
exclusive sound effect in Hollywood was all over town.
Sound guys were calling each other up and playing it
over the phone. *Hey, Clyde, just listen to what I got!* An
editor at Compact Video even played it for me. No
question about it. After all this time, Goofy finally was
over the falls.

Fish Story

One of the more common homilies in the professional writing game is that the writer should know firsthand what he's talking about before he puts his fingers to the keyboard. You hear it all the time, said one way or another: Louis L'Amour, the Western writer who killed off an entire troop of cheap scribblers who copied from each other, bragged that if he wrote of a wilderness place or a water hole, he'd personally rode those trails and tasted of that water. In the 1920s, travel writer Richard Halliburton made a decent living swimming the Hellespont and sneaking around the moonlit Taj Mahal and then penning his adventures in The Royal Road To Romance and other florid travel tomes. George Plimpton, of course, did somewhat the same, living the life of an NFL footballer for his Paper Tiger. I once directed Plimpton in a taped segment for the Disney Channel, and, believe me, it was a stretch to imagine that thin-shouldered little pip-squeak with his William F. Buckley-like English dialect darting around the gridiron with the beefy likes of Alex Karras and Roger Brown after his skinny little butt.

Even actors who wait tables or sell suits can study real people. It's somewhat harder for advertising creative people, who so quickly become locked in their own fantasies that they are often accused of living in ivory towers. In that world of chromium leopards it is a badge of honor to have mingled with the common herd. Burnett Creative Head Norm Muse always bragged he started his climb to fame selling pots and pans door-to-door. And Hal Cone, one of the brighter and more popular Creative Directors to ply his trade at the Burnett Agency, used to tell his young writers that they had to get out of the office at least once a year to actually *sell real stuff to real people.* Hal practiced what he preached, every year working nights in a deli for three or four weeks before Christmas.

Hal knew it is dangerous spending your adult life in marketing; your ads and commercials run, the product sells, therefore, you must have done it. Pretty soon, you're explaining the latest sales increases in terms of the brilliant creative work you did. And then you start to believe it. It's too easy to forget William Kellogg's rueful comment, "I know half my advertising budget isn't working--I just don't know which half."

Face it, advertising is a frustrating business, not only for the writers who have to come up with interesting ads where the only subtext is "buy this product". It's frustrating for marketing, new biz and research as well. It's the original uncertainty business. You can do a great campaign and the client makes 150 million bucks. You do it a couple of times, and sometimes you can get the urge to do it for yourself.

While very few marketers have the guts and the gumption to take that one additional step and put their money where their hyperbolas are, my friend Buck never had that problem. Today, he ruefully tells his story as if he wishes he'd taken a different course.

Clear-eyed and decisive, Buck brought his college marketing degrees and his U.S. Marine Corps officer experience to the ad game. I met him in Detroit, where we both worked on the Ford Corporate account. He was an account exec. I was the head of broadcast production. I left for Hollywood to do show biz stuff, and

Buck went to a big ad agency in Philly. A couple of years later, he called me. He was very excited. He and an advertising account exec pal of his had bought *Fisherman's Hardware,* a well-known sports fishing store in Long Beach, California. It was an interesting plan, and conservative by most standards. They both had ad exec jobs in Los Angeles, which they would keep at least for the immediate future. Their thinking was that this fish store investment was going to be a lucrative sideline, and once it caught on big, they would quit their regular jobs as they expanded the *Fisherman's Hardware* franchise throughout California, then the western states, and then nationally. It couldn't miss because they were going to use all the wisdom and special knowledge they had picked up during their years in advertising. Who better to turn this single store with its established local name and solid reputation into a national brand? I didn't know what to think. He didn't want advice, he was full of confidence. So I wished him luck and went back to my keyboard, pounding out brilliant concepts to sell other people's products.

A couple of years went by before Buck and I talked again. Much had gone on in the interim. His partner had gotten religion and left for Alabama to produce and distribute a line of inspirational musical tapes (today he's a multi-millionaire). Buck still owned the one *Fisherman's Hardware* store in Long Beach. Now he wanted to put temporary fishing tackle stores in shopping malls over the Christmas season, and so make a killing on the Holiday trade. That year I wasn't doing much in the way of taking over Hollywood, and, remembering Hal Cone's advice, I agreed to run one of Buck's outlets.

We took over a deserted store in the Sherman Oaks Galleria. We called it *Something Fishy.* The first thing I noticed was that the mall people were charging something outrageous--thousands of dollars per week-- for the space. It bothered Buck, too, but he said we would just raise the prices on everything we sold. As people bought out of impulse during Christmas, they would buy from us anyway, no matter the markup.

We were sitting on a nearby bench while the mall employees hung up our store banner, *Something Fishy*. I asked Buck how things were going.

He gave me a harried look, "It has been an incredible experience."

I reminded him that incredible wasn't necessarily good.

He smiled sadly. "You remember how I was a few years ago. I was going to do powerful image newspaper ads that persuaded folks they had to come to *Fisherman's Hardware*."

"Yeah. I remember," I said.

"I found out that to buy the ad space in the newspapers I needed to co-op with my suppliers. That meant my ads ended up looking just as crapped up with reels and rods and creepy-crawly worms as everybody else's."

"Bummer," I said.

"Yeah," he agreed. "But it gets worse. Then I found out that the margin of profit in our store wasn't enough to hire a manager. So I had to give up my day job at the agency. Today I spend most of my life running around to suppliers, holding off creditors and trying to keep my staff happy."

"Double bummer," I said.

"It gets worse. Then I found out that the sports chains and the discount department stores were killing us. Fishermen are like the fish they go after--they'll feed like crazy when the price is right. My life has slowly become one big cash flow problem. I'm always forced to put on a big sale to get back at least part of my money so I can buy more stock and hold another sale."

"Oh," I said, convinced I'd heard the last of the bad news. But Buck had more.

"The other problem is, we paid way too much for the business in the first place. We can't service that six-figure loan and pay ourselves anything."

"So why are we doing this Christmas thing?"

"If I can just make some fat profits maybe I can get back on my feet."

I had my doubts, but I didn't say anything. *Something Fishy* opened the last week in November and I sat there like a bored sea bass, waiting for minnows to come along. Hal was right; I did learn a lot about people and selling. Unfortunately for Buck, selling fishing tackle in malls wasn't much different from selling it at his Long Beach store. True, we were able to mark things up so high that we could drive over to discount stores and buy reels, mark them up 30% and still sell them. And true, schools of shoppers did show up to nibble at the merchandise...but they didn't bite in big enough droves to pay for that awful rent. *Something Fishy* was still a financial drain, only serving to tighten the noose around Buck's neck.

He refused to throw in the reel, and so we limped on through the month while he frantically balanced creditors and the dwindling stocks in both our stores with his shrinking pile of cash. I hung around a few days after Christmas for the clearance sale; we had a few bites at 20% off, a few more at 30% off, and a few more at 40%--but the feeding frenzy didn't start until Buck hand-painted and pasted up a big red sign HALF PRICE SALE--EVERYTHING MUST GO! The minute that sign went up in the window, a swarm of shoppers of every age, size and description appeared as if by magic. Some even apologized for doing their next year's Holiday shopping early, some were grim and swift in picking through the merchandise, but together they quickly bought out the store. And a few of them even haggled Buck down from 50%. *Hey, we wanted to get rid of the stuff, didn't we?*

Something Fishy only sank Buck deeper in the money pit, and the entire venture ended badly for him. He finally had to sell the *Fisherman's Hardware* outlet for less than half of what he paid for it. He was a straight-up guy about it; most businessmen would have declared belly-up and swam away, but Buck worked out a deal with the creditors and spent the next ten years of his life paying them off.

You've got to hand it to him. He had an idea, and where most ad guys would have just let it itch, he actually went out and scratched it. The whole experience didn't kill him, and he went back to the Detroit ad world where he did some really big things on the Buick line.

But if you're a copywriter or even a big-time Creative Director, maybe the next time you're groping for the adjectives to hype some incredible new product and you start longing for the big profits you might get by hawking your very own product, you might do well to remember my friend Buck and his experience with the big fish store that got away.

Pass Me the Shrunken Conan

Phil Mendez and I were having lunch at a little place crammed with small tables with black-and-white checkered tablecloths. As I remember, this place was located at the crest of Pass Avenue behind Universal Studios. Phil being the ebullient guy he is, he'd already charmed the maitre d' and the waitress and was walking from table to table, working the crowd, which was mostly production people from the various small studios and independent film shops nearby.

Phil looks like a cross between a Greek barkeep and a Negro fisherman. He's big and burly, with a whiskery face, a great laugh and a basketful of voices and impersonations, like a high-speed Robin Williams caught in Pavarotti's big body. Needless to say, he's always been a natural born storyteller, a quality that comes in handy when selling his story ideas and projects to the studios and the networks. When he's on, an incredible range of voices and personalities spills out and there's no getting the real Phil back, sometimes for hours. He will be absolutely unpredictable, 100 percent pure Phil Mendez, a Hollywood original.

He's also one of the world's great artists, and a Disney-trained animator, to boot. You may know him for Kissyfur, a Saturday Morning Kid's show about a little bear living in the swamps of the Deep South. That was Phil's baby.

I had written a few short pieces for him for <u>Star Street</u>, a syndicated animation series he and a mellow-voiced guy with the unlikely name of Bunker Jenkins were producing for some Dutch people. Then I adapted a novel called <u>Hobberdy Dick</u> to screenplay format for them for a Japanese company. And now I was working with Phil on a feature film, <u>Sindbad's Dreamquest</u>, for a joint Finnish-Iranian film company. The writing and the storyboarding were not going well for either of us, as the Finns and their southern neighbors really wanted total authorship for themselves. It's a common problem; everybody thinks they are a writer. They try to strip your ideas, steal the format, and go it alone, hoping to end up with the credits. The Writers Guild has an arbitration process to stop some of this, but it doesn't apply to animation. Animation is still, generally speaking, a dirty, unprotected business for the workingman. No way these guys were in my league, much less Phil's...but they had the money, and that's a common enough story out here in Hollywood.

Anyway, there's a whole lure written about animators and the things they've created on the backs of menus and on napkins and tablecloths around L.A. Sometimes restaurant owners have them framed and hung in their eateries, or sold at auction. Once when I was waiting for Phil at a chichi croissant palace called Chez Nous in Toluca Lake, Phil was slouched over in a far corner, hiding so he could draw a not-too-kind picture of me on a napkin. It's me alright, but my eyes are squinting and he scribbled in a balloon over my head, saying, "I write...You read...you pay."

Now, as we waited for our chicken salads, Phil suddenly turned over the paper mat underneath his plate and started to sketch a scene from <u>The Black Cauldron</u> on the clear back side of the paper. This scene had a couple of cowardly knaves falling before the majesty of

204

the evil Horned King. The King was huge and massive, with the arms and torso of a bodybuilder; he had a puckery grin like he'd been eating sauerkraut. I only knew one guy who had a smile like that, and Phil confirmed my suspicions when he drew a balloon over the King's head and wrote, "We are going to pump-you-up!" In another second, Phil bounded up and presented his drawing to Arnold Schwarzenegger, who was sitting in the seat directly behind me.

This was before Arnie took to politics, but what really amazed me was the downsizing that went on in my mind as I looked at him. I kept thinking, "This must be Arnie's little brother. This can't be Conan, this can't be the Terminator!" I'd heard all the stories about Alan Ladd, and how at 5 foot 7 inches, he'd had to play the great western hero Shane while walking on the milk carton-like boxes film crews call "apple boxes". But Arnie wasn't just short, he was *little*, at least when compared to his bulging screen image. Now don't get me wrong, he was in great shape. He made both Phil and me look like we'd better get right down to Racquetball World for all the aerobics our hearts could stand.

We didn't really have much to say. Arnold accepted Phil's drawing, and he seemed to get a kick out of it. But, for once, Phil seemed genuinely starstruck and tongue-tied. As I wasn't too interested in testing the little big man's knowledge of English, I did a few polite nods and turned back to my chicken salad. We needed Robin Williams to keep the conversation going. Where is the Fisher King when you need him?

On the way back over the hill to Phil's three-room animation studio, I mentioned how struck I was at Schwarzenegger's diminutive size.

"What," Phil laughed, "You thought he'd be six foot nine like in <u>Terminator</u>?"

"Yeah, I guess so." I couldn't keep the disappointment from creeping into my voice.

"Nothing's sacred any more, eh Johnny-boy?" Phil commiserated, talking like a Brooklyn wise guy.

I was really in a funk. I sighed, not up for more of Phil's lightning mind-shifts into other people's personas. "Something like that. Who can you believe in when you find out Conan the Barbarian only weighs 190 pounds? Maybe next we'll hear that Clint Eastwood wears a girdle."

With that, Phil laughed his real laugh, the great, hearty boomer that always seemed to put everything in perspective. "Hey," he said, "This is *Hollywood*. At least he wasn't a dwarf."

Teddy Post's War

He walks with a limp and an ornate cane, and when he's been on his feet all day you can see the pain in his eyes. But you don't say anything--nobody on the set dares say anything--because this is the same Ted Post who nearly lost his leg on a beach in Italy in World War II.

They dressed him for pre-op, which means they swabbed him down with alcohol in the big tent where they were hacking off maimed limbs. When the saw-bones bent over to have a look at his face, to see if this one might survive the operation, Teddy grabbed his dog tags, staring hard at the name stamped there.

"If you cut off my leg," he said grimly to the man he'd pulled close to his lips, "I'll spend the rest of my life until I find you. And then I'll hack *your* leg off."

"But you'll die if we don't," the doctor said, prying his dog tags from Teddy's fingers and pulling back to a safer distance.

"I'd rather be dead. It's my choice. You do it my way."

"But the bones are all crushed," the doctor begged.

"I'll just be a little shorter on that side," Teddy said.

That's the kind of guy he is. Legendary Teddy Post. He's a Hollywood legend, too, a director whose list of television and movie credits spans four generations. What director worked with Clint Eastwood on both <u>Hang 'Em High</u> and <u>Magnum Force</u>? What director did both the pilot show for <u>Perry Mason</u> and the pilot for <u>Cagney & Lacey</u>? What director has done <u>Gunsmoke</u>, <u>The Fred Astaire Show</u>, <u>Twilight Zone</u>, <u>Peyton Place</u>, and <u>Columbo</u>? Teddy Post, of course.

When I heard he was teaching a Master Director's Class at the Directors Guild, I called down to see if I could get in. The course was limited to 12, "by invitation only", and was already filled. But at the last minute somebody dropped out and I was in.

This was in the spring of 1985. There would be eight sessions in all, four hours every Saturday morning for two months. Each of us would be expected to direct at least two dramatic pieces of a five to ten minute length with two or more actors. At that time I was adapting my novel <u>Crazyhead</u> to screenplay format, so I thought maybe I could try out some of the scenes on the class.

I knew Teddy had directed <u>Go Tell the Spartans</u>, which was one of the few Vietnam War pictures to be produced up until that time. I went out and rented it, and, for me, it played a bit like a lot of war movies I'd seen somewhere else before. You had your stiff officer types, your sacrificial lambs, your war that nobody understands, and your "sensitive" type writer-hero, the scribe, who is aware of it all. Of course, there is a certain universality to all warfare, particularly as Hollywood throws it up on the silver screen: The blood and guts, the madness, the wrong people always die, and the Greek Chorus wails to let us know it.

Beyond this sameness, I have noticed *certain trends* to the serious books and movies. The big guys, Crane, Conrad, Hemingway, and Heller dictate the form and even the content. Then come the rest of the guys, particularly the film guys, who ply their craft with a certain degree of imitation. Adaptation, we call it. Francis Ford Coppola wants to make a statement about the war, so he updates Conrad. Teddy Post wants to make a statement about the war so he updates Crane and Heller.

At any rate, I'd been amazed and dumbfounded by my own experiences in the army, both stateside and in Vietnam. I'd seen insubordination beyond all belief, astounding greed, ignorance and petty behavior...as well as occasional individual acts of sacrifice and heroism. I didn't know if my own writing was minor-key Hemingway or pulp-Heller, and I didn't care. I was just trying to get it down on paper.

The first time I tried a Vietnam scene on the class, I did a little story where my four heroes, American cryptographer/linguists with top secret clearances, are sent outside Saigon to work with Vietnamese Intelligence in a fairly unsecured area. Three of the four Americans spend their time fooling around and making fun of the war effort. But their mood changes once they realize their room is bugged.

Teddy Post's Master Director's Class jumped on my offering like vultures on dead meat. I could have withstood that; they tore apart everything everybody did, seeing it as part of their job, a new meaning to the idea of class participation. But what really depressed me was the way Teddy rejected the piece. He kept telling me, "Soldiers just don't act that way."

I went back and reviewed Go Tell the Spartans. It was, at heart, an anti-war film, the story of what happens when the U.S. military high command foolishly insists on building a distant outpost in an area where the enemy has massive strength (and so is a parable about our foolish participation in the war as a whole). In Spartans, the outpost is saved from instant annihilation by the presence of old war hand Burt Lancaster, who recognizes doom is coming and prepares the men for the fight of their lives (deaths). The characters are fairly stet; the gnarly officer who ruined his career by dropping his pants at the wrong time, the young sensitive writer-recruit, the smattering of drunks and dopers sure to "get theirs" when the shit comes raining down, the handful of inscrutable Vietnamese "friendlies" who either prove to be loyal or deceitful. *What the hell was wrong with my stuff?*

It took a full week's effort to prep a scene for that class. After selecting the scene, there were casting, blocking out the action, and rehearsals. While my classmates tore each other's work apart with abandon, I noticed there were openings every week; these guys weren't so eager to get their own stuff up on the stage. This was a big opportunity for me, and I resolved to do something every time there was an opening. In a sense, I guess you could say I *saved* the class, because some weeks I was the only person who had prepared a scene. Without me, there would have been nothing to tear apart.

That aside, the course was great. Teddy showed me a hundred things; how to pull down an actor who was dominating the scene when he wasn't supposed to, how to shift the mood and the tempo, how to color the scene to make it say what you wanted. And my fellow students were giving me lessons on accepting criticism. A guy like me *should* be made to eat humble pie every once in a while. It makes me bearable in polite company. I could handle that--but one problem really nagged at me.

Teddy still didn't seem to like anything I did. He just sat there, frowning at the behavior of my four mad heroes. Was I being too presumptuous, performing my own stuff instead of taking scenes from plays and scripts written by others? Did I have some terrible blind spot? Was my stuff just *bad*? I kept coming back to his first reaction to my first piece. *Soldiers just don't act that way.*

For my final piece, I resolved to let out all the stops. I had a scene which takes place in the "Puzzle Palace", the top secret intelligence headquarters of the National Security Agency. Three of our four heroes, irreverent as ever, are goofing off, and, in doing so, they manage to infuriate their superior officer. But there is more to the scene; there has been a tragic, yet amusing incident. A drunken sergeant has fallen into a giant pulper used to dispose of the tons of top secret waste paper which must be discarded each day. One of our happy-go-lucky characters is going to use this incident to trick the army into giving his friend his dream--an assignment in Vietnam.

After my actors completed the scene, which was somewhat longer than the previous ones I'd done, there was the usual stunned silence, then hands shot up all over the room. Besides Teddy, I had one other nemesis, a ramrod straight assistant director who had been in Vietnam almost a decade. He'd started as an enlisted man and risen in the ranks until he was finally field-promoted to officer. This guy's hand shot up like a gun, and Teddy nodded in his direction.

"The problem with this piece," the guy said, "is that I don't like any of these soldiers."

"That's just your experience," I fired back. "You're a pretty rare animal, yourself." One of the big things I was learning was to be hard-crusted, and to fight for my ideas.

"How's that?" He looked genuinely puzzled.

"Well, you started as a private and ended up a Captain."

"What the hell difference does that make?"

"No matter what else you think about the war, that is one reason for you to like it, to be on the side of discipline and rigidity and *The War Effort*. Suppose you'd started as a Captain and ended up a Corporal? I'm sure you wouldn't feel the same."

There was a titter from the group. The guy looked like he was going to say something else, but thought better of it and sat down.

Teddy cleared his throat from the back of the room. "I have the same problem with this that I have with the other war scenes you've done. These characters aren't believable."

I'd had it with my Master Director. I'm sure the impatience showed in my voice, "You've got me, Teddy. I really don't know what the hell you're talking about."

He lurched to his feet, "Look, you're not the only one who knows about Vietnam!"

"Didn't say I was. I said I don't know what you're getting at. You keep saying the same things, but I don't understand them."

"I know about war! I was in World War II! And I did what is arguably the best movie about Vietnam to this date! And I tell you, soldiers don't act the way yours do. The way they mouthed off to that officer?! They'd have been in the brig--or shot!"

It was suddenly clearer to me. "Soldiers you knew didn't act that way *in your war*, Teddy. World War II. The war to save the world from Hitler. We didn't have your motivation in the Nam War."

"The army doesn't change that much!"

"How would you know?--you never were in Nam. You haven't been in the army in 40 years!"

"That's *your* opinion! You don't have to go to Vietnam to know about Vietnam!"

"Well, it helps, Teddy."

My nemesis was on his feet again, the tall geek who'd risen from private to Captain, "Maybe your war experience *narrowed* your opinion rather than *broadened* it!"

"Right. The real thing makes you more ignorant. Where do you come up with this stuff?"

"It could have...", he insisted.

"Hey, guys. All I know is, I went and I saw for myself. It wasn't like Crane, it wasn't like Conrad, it wasn't like Hemingway, and it wasn't like Heller, and it wasn't like Teddy Post. It was like what it was. Imagine. A war where--arguably--as many soldiers saved their own lives by disobeying orders as by obeying them."

"That's not a war, that's an abomination.

"What war is not?"

It went on a while longer, but there really wasn't a resolution. There never is, when Americans chew over the Nam war. The North Vietnamese are the only ones who can see it clearly, their images all crystal-clear in the bright wash of victory.

For our part, Teddy, the other guy and I were just three guys arguing about our wars. Win or lose, war is always a harsh reality for those who live through it. It kills the losers; but it marks, it defines, the survivors for the rest of their lives. Teddy gave up his physical well-being for his war, and I gave up my innocence for mine. We both saw pain, and terror and craziness and death. We both had been seared by the hot breath of the war god, and in the aftermath, we each clung to our own experiences, to what got us through. For Teddy, it was discipline and iron will. For me, it was imagination and risk-taking. No wonder we didn't see eye to eye.

The conversation drifted to other things. This was our last session, and Teddy did a sort of a review and a wrap-up of the class accomplishments. I looked at the wall over his head, letting his voice drone on. The experience had been worth the effort, but I was glad it was over. It was time to move on.

The Film Lover

Do you ever long to write a book, get into poetry, take great nature photos or do a movie? In spite of all the crazy and absurd obstacles to actually doing what you want in the creative world, I cannot find strong enough words to encourage you. Maybe you are a creative genius, and maybe not. But in the long run, what does it matter? If it fulfills your dream, why not? And, there's always the long shot chance, maybe you really are a creative wonder, and maybe somebody who counts and who can actually do something about it will agree, and your career will take off like a rocket.

Maybe you think it's the original impossible dream to become a filmmaker. But consider this: The great nuclear physicist, theoretic cosmic thinker and bongo drummer Richard Feynman once said, *There is very little difference between the average ordinary but interested person and the so-called expert.* Believe me, professionals all over Hollywood go to bed every night praying the so-called "little people" (you and me) never figure that one out. *Viva la difference,* as Maurice Chevalier used to say about another, but similar, matter. If they could, the movie moguls would take guys like Feynman, stick their feet in tubs of Quik-Dry cement and use them in their next gangland flick.

My old army buddy Charlie loved the movies, and he went to see them a lot. Being Italian, he loved <u>The Godfather</u> series and anything with Joe Pesci in it. But he would also attend romances with his wife, and action/horror stuff with his daughter.

"That was a good movie," he would say of something like <u>Aliens</u>. "They handled the monster right, I thought."

Charlie lived in San Joe where he did well as a mortgage broker, but his heart and soul was in the cinema business. Nothing so out of the ordinary here...so far. Charlie saw pictures the way we all do, and he made the same kinds of comments we all make about them.

Then what, you may ask, makes this Charlie character any different from the rest of us poor saps?

Well, I would answer, two things, maybe. First, he really did have a well-developed filmic sense, that special something that tells you a scene is playing wrong even if it has Jack Nicholson and Meryl Streep in it. And second, he had resolved that, no matter what it took, he was going to get into the movie business.

He finally decided to film a script developed by his brother-in-law and a friend who wrote a food column for the <u>San Jose Mercury</u>. It was called <u>Lockdown</u>, and it was a low-budget cop-buddy story.

It was pretty hack stuff, and worse, there were five or six holes in the script that you could drive a getaway truck through. I told Charlie as much and we had a big argument about it. He said he knew it wasn't all that great, but you had to start somewhere. This was the script, and they were going to start now. At the time I'd already worked for over a decade for the studios and I'd seen every way in the world not to make a movie. I didn't understand the urgency.

"Two weeks," I argued. "Just take two weeks and fix the script."

"I don't have two weeks, Kha," he said, using my old nickname from the Nam war. "We gotta shoot now."

I softened a little (it doesn't come easy for me), and told him I'd look in on him every now and then, to see how it was going. To tell the truth, I felt more responsible than I'm saying. I'd introduced Charlie to the low-budget director/cameraman who was going to shoot Lockdown. This low-budget guy was a Hollywood contact of mine, not Charlie's.

Charlie raised $150,000 and shooting started immediately. They had most of it in the can before they ran out of money. The director/cameraman still owed Charlie a few key scenes--explosions, car blowups, the things so dear to the hearts of low-budget indy filmmakers and essential to the foreign-market buyers-- but the money was gone.

And here was where, as a first-time producer, Charlie proved to be somewhat of a *phe-nom*, as in *The Kid's a phe-nom,* like they used to say back in the streets of his native Bayonne, New Jersey. He held cast and crew together with the strength of his personality. He paid starvation wages while he fished for additional financing. He cheered from the sidelines. No matter how long a setup took, no matter how late at night, Charlie was the last one to leave the set.

He even arranged for distribution rights, making a shrewd deal that would assure post-production money to finish the film, and eventually put the picture in the black...if he could only finish principal photography. It was at about this time that I put in a call to my filmmaker acquaintance, the writer-director I'd hooked up with Charlie in the first place. My voice, I remember, was low and troubled, and as the conversation went on, slowly sank into something bordering on menace. I don't know why I made it go that way. Charlie was a close friend, and sometimes blood and water are just as thick. My dialogue was full of insinuations, of family, of blood ties and connections. After all, Charlie was Sicilian. The last

216

thing I said was something to the effect of, "You owe my friend and you're holding out. You don't really know what you're playing around with. Now, I suggest in the strongest possible way, that you finish what you promised." On his end of the line, the guy started to babble angrily, and I hung up on him.

Of course, he called Charlie right away, complaining about my attitude, shouting that who the hell was I to tell him what to do? Charlie, never a dummy, played the small coin I'd tossed him, telling him, "If it wasn't for Kha, you wouldn't be on this film. You wouldn't even know me."

Charlie, too, hung up on him. A few weeks later the final shots were finished. Principal photography was completed, Charlie's deal was formalized with the distributor, and Lockdown was a real motion picture.

And just in time. Mortgage brokers, by the nature of their business, make a lot of enemies. And there was this third thing that I may not have mentioned about him: though he was a long way from the streets of Bayonne, he hadn't completely left the flavor of his old neighborhood behind him. Charlie, who grew up street-smart and worked his own way through college, never was one to shy away from a walk on the wild side. All of which at least hints at why, one day a few weeks after he had completed principal photography, a young punk wearing a Porsche baseball cap and an expensive leather jacket walked up to him, pulled out a pistol and shot him. He died late that night, leaving his family, his friends and many in San Jose in a state of shock and mourning.

As for Lockdown, the script problems didn't get fixed on the set as Charlie had hoped. But filmmaking has always been the art of the possible dream, and Charlie made that first dream come true when he took $250,000 and made it look like $2 million on the screen.

I wish he would have lived to do some more. It was what he was born to do. Sometimes I try to imagine what would have happened if one of the biggies had handed him 30 million dollars like they routinely give the local Tinseltown thieves and charlatans. A little more time and he would have been a wonder, his name maybe even a household word like Coppola or Spielberg. If you don't believe me, look it up for yourself in one of those film compendiums. <u>Lockdown</u>, starring Richard Lynch, Cris DeRose, Elizabeth Kaitan and Joe Estevez and produced by my old army buddy Charlie.

Somewhere Over the Rainbow

My dad used to say, "True friends are like jewels--so very rare you'll be lucky to find two or three of them your entire lifetime." I hadn't thought of that in a long time, until Gani called again last night.

He called at nearly 11 o'clock, his excitement breaking through his heavy Filipino accent.

"D'john," he said, "D'john! I got your beeg-a break! Dis time, it's for sure!" He hadn't called for three or four years, since the disastrous <u>Tunnel Rats</u> project. Gani is a true independent filmmaker, one of the last of the do-it-yourselfers, and the <u>Rats</u> film collapsed around our ears like the tunnels of Cu Chi themselves when they were pounded by American B-52's during the Nam War. It had seemed like such a sure thing. The huts for the Vietnamese village had already been built on a rolling Luzon hillside speckled with palm trees. And somebody had actually constructed a maze of tunnels in a basketball gym outside of Manila. Hollywood magic. Gani was going to produce. I was supposed to do a rewrite and direct. But the fly in the ointment was the Philippine moneyman, who had personally written the script. He didn't really want a rewrite; he wanted me to fix his outrageously bad grammar, and he wanted me to do it for free. I took a walk, and Gani was upset with me at the time. But a few months later the same moneyman stiffed him for almost sixty grand on another picture, and so Gani came around to my point of view.

Somebody else did eventually make Tunnel Rats. I'm not sure who; the world of indy filmmaking is a potboiler on the low-budget end, where action/adventure, horror, gang violence, exploitation and war films are ground out like cheap sausages. Ideas are stolen, lifetime friends knife each other over who gets what, and projects die and reappear in new life forms like vampires rising from the coffin. Come to think of it, the world of studio big-budget production isn't much different. The numbers are all in seven or eight figures instead of five or six, the criminals you meet are more pompous and polished, and occasionally some of the writing and acting is a little better, but that's about it.

Anyway, back in the early 60's, Gani was a native of the Philippines shooting documentaries in Vietnam for the U.S. Information Services. After it got too hot to roam freely around the Mekong Delta and the Central Highlands, he gave up the rigorous doc-a-week routine and came to the States where he went back to school. He earned his Masters from the prestigious USC film school, graduating around the same time as Francis Ford Coppola and George Lucas.

I met him in the late seventies, during the period when he was working by day as a much-maligned assistant film editor at Disney. In those days, the studio was hardly integrated, and Gani, who was as squat, gnarled and gruff as the original troll-under-the-bridge, was the butt of a thousand jokes. The only reason they kept him around was that he was assisting for a rabid Jehovah's Witness, a doom-and-gloomer nobody else wanted to work for. Imagine what it must have been like; you're trying to cut bright and happy new trailers for delightfully animated classics like Pinocchio or Cinderella with your boss constantly reminding you to get your shit in order because the final holocaust is at hand. But Gani was resilient; if he minded, he was careful to keep it to himself. He saw the other editors in the shop as limited men with limited talent and limited dreams. He himself alone among them was *a filmmaker*. After all, he confided to me, *he had an entire studio in his basement.*

I never thought much about it while I was at Disney. I thought Gani was a great cutter; and when a slot for a full editor came available, I supported him for it. After Barry Lorie came in as new publicity head and I got canned for being knowledgeable and in the way, I remembered Gani was always talking about the setup he had at home, and so I hired him to cut some Green Spot soft drink commercials I'd shot. I must say, I wasn't prepared for what I walked into.

Gani not only had a few moviolas, he was the first editor at Disney to use a flatbed editing system. He'd bought it himself at a cost of over $20,000 and set it up in his basement. Cramped in the five or six rooms under his house in the old Silverlake neighborhood in L.A., he also had two 35 mm interlock projectors and a wall-sized projection screen, ten 35 mm sound-transfer machines for sound mixing (they are about six feet tall, and wide as a person), a looping stage complete with cement slab and sand and gravel pits for making special effects, and an equipment room overflowing with cameras, sound recording and lighting equipment.

The walls and even the ceiling screamed with huge posters of the features he'd line-produced, co-produced and executive produced over the years. These were movies nobody in the mainstream had ever heard of, part of a thriving industry supported by overseas money and film distribution systems. "Uhh, yeah," he'd say, shrugging and tremendously pleased that I'd asked about his private little kingdom, "That's A Bullet For Your Music, starring Johnny Ramos. He's a beega-shot in the Philippines. I shoot four week here in L.A., and a couple of weeks in Manila. I finish th' whole picture right here, in my basement. Anybody from the islands wants to shoot a picture in Hollywood, they come see me first, 'cause I do it cheap and good."

Gani is one of those rare, almost mythological finds in Hollywood--or anywhere else, I guess--a true friend. He's trying to get me that biggest break of all in Tinseltown, my first feature picture to direct. He is sure that one day soon it will happen. And so he says, his voice booming over the phone, "D'john, this is it! We now 95% there! We just need one, maybe two name on the paper! You and me--we gonna be in the Philippines in one month! You got to believe me, D'john!"

And, you know, I do. In spite of all the institutionalized graft and corruption, in spite of the lying, the cheating and stealing you see around this town, I do believe in Gani. Because this is Hollywood, the place where every once in a while, if you try hard enough and never ever give up, the dreams you dream really do come true.

How to Not Write Your First Novel

Have you read that book <u>The Discoverers</u>? It's an encouraging historical account of the many wrong and the few right turns the mighty movers and shakers of our civilization took on the way to creating the "modern" society we have today. Water-drip and candle clocks and heavier-than-air flying contraptions and Columbus miscalculating the size of the earth by 25%...I found it encouraging because I figure, if everybody else can make such outrageous miscalculations, there's hope yet for me as a novelist.

Baring my soul, I can reveal all now: The noble quest of my youth--and, indeed, my early middle age-- was always to write the Great American Novel. It was my dream, my lifework. Writing, producing and directing advertising commercials, documentaries, television specials and motion pictures was stuff I did just to hone my skills and keep bread on the table. At heart, I was a *novelist*.

My first enormous miscalculation (which I made at the very start) was to assume, as I'd always been told as a college English Major, that you can't learn anything from Creative Writing courses. I began as we all do, with the blank page. But instead of taking the advice of those who knew, I unwittingly took every twisted turn and blind alley explored by the legions of failed and broken scribblers who had gone before me.

My initial outrageous idea was to combine poetry and prose, which I did in a long, self-indulgent tome called The Messi Bessi that I suspect was mostly about my own uniqueness. Rejected by agents *en masse*, this was followed by Umbleburger in D.C., a story about an idealistic young man who goes to Washington and there is devoured by the various powers that be. Although one New York agent, Jay Garon, said I showed promise and should continue to write, there was no sale.

I plunged into my work with a vengeance. By this time I was in Detroit, in the light of day running Grey Advertising's commercial production department. Ahh, but by night, I wrote in a damp cellar in Royal Oak, Michigan, with my feet wrapped in blankets and the lonely crackle of an electric heater for solace. The manuscripts began to pile up around me. I was learning that poetry may have been great for Virgil, but Random House wasn't buying that format anymore. By this time, I had a small stack of novel manuscripts, short stories and screenplays.

I'd been in Vietnam during the war as a linguist/translator with a Top Secret clearance working in military intelligence. I felt I had some interesting things to say, and this topic could lead to my capturing the mythical Holy Grail of American scribes, The Great American Novel.

My first attempt to do something on Vietnam, In The Interest Of National Security, was finished in the early 70's. It topped out at 700 single-spaced pages. In a warped attempt to catch some editor's eye, I typed the entire manuscript in *italics*. There were some encouraging remarks, but in general the response from editors was so scathing that I set Vietnam aside for a number of years. *Single-spaced italics--this man should be boiled in oil!!* My small trunk was now nearly filled with experimental novels, screenplays, short stories and other writing projects.

By the early 80's I'd written, sold and produced commercials, documentaries, educationals, jingles, kid's television programming, cable and television specials-- but I still hadn't sold that first novel. By now the first trunk was filled with unsold manuscripts, and I was starting on the second.

Sometime in the early 80's, in reviewing all the work I'd done, I ran across a pile of old letters from agents and publishers. All in all, a couple of them weren't that bad. *A powerful and unique style*, one of them said. *Shows real promise*, another praised. *Send us anything you do--not on Vietnam!*, a third advised. Bottom line, the *quality of my rejections* was getting better.

Encouraged, I set out to analyze more closely what I'd been doing wrong. The Messi Bessi and my other early poetic/dramatic works like Crystals of Mud and Bits of Glass had shown flashes of good writing. But the form was so far from convention that most agents and editors didn't know what to do with me. My later works, particularly my Vietnam manuscript, seemed closer and closer to what might sell...but they still were long and wordy, at their best like the old Thomas Wolfe in You Can't Go Home Again, at their worst like a sloshy Dylan Thomas.

One night, while pondering over my 700 single-spaced pages of Vietnam material, I came to the decision that in that one volume I had enough material to write six or seven novels, all tied by character and place. I extracted the materials for what I saw as the third of the series, a story about Mad Denny Haller, a fiery-tempered G.I. who's been in-country too long. Mad Denny's a fallen angel, a tainted *Terry-And-The-Pirates*, a sort of modern day Bogart. And just when he tries to get out of petty dope dealing, he slips into the big time. I called it Crazyhead and sent out 545 double-spaced pages to various agents--and was once again solidly rejected. I couldn't figure it. I'd finally gotten the plot to build perfectly, the pacing humming along at an exciting level, the characters interesting and involving--in short, I felt I had (in the lingo of the book biz) *the pages turning*. But still, no sale.

Five or six years went by. Finally, one day in the parking lot of the Denny's restaurant on Sunset, I found myself complaining about my plight to Erich Van Lowe, another writer who was working with me on a new show idea for animator Phil Mendez. By now, I was ready to forget the Holy Grail, I just wanted to get published before I died. Wild-eyed and arms waving, lanky Erich and I must have looked like two drug dealers arguing over the prices. He was a black guy, very bright and excitable, who had taken some courses on writing from USC. He'd written and sold two paperback novels about a black Dracula, done a lot of kid's Saturday Morning cartoon stuff and now was about to head to New York to work on the Bill Cosby Show. After I poured out my whole sad tale, he looked at me like I was the last of the Neanderthal writers.

"So far," he said, "from what you've told me, over the last twenty years you have broken every basic writer's rule ever invented. The truth is, no one tries to write the Great American Novel any more, because, even if you did write it, they wouldn't recognize it, and even if they did, they certainly wouldn't publish it, because nobody would read it."

"Great," I muttered, looking around for a rusty piece of sharp metal or a sliver of glass to slit my wrists.

"Look, pal," Erich said, "First rule, the publishers are all whores. ALL of them. There isn't an idealist left in the whole pack. Second, editors don't edit anymore. So if you don't give them something *ready for galleys*, forget it. Nobody encourages young writers along anymore. Editors don't edit, they *package and market*. And third, all books are published in *categories*. So, if you want to be published, you gotta *write in categories*.

226

Go look in a bookstore, they're all there, plain as day: Sci-Fi, Horror, Romance, Westerns, Mysteries. If it ain't in there, you ain't gonna sell it. You write anything else, *it's gonna fall through the cracks.* Sorry, white boy, but them's the hard facts."

Looking back over the long string of agents, publishers and editors I'd alternately confused, upset and outraged, and the huge stack of rejections I'd accumulated over the years, I had to agree with Erich. "Okay, I admit it. In twenty years, I haven't done anything that works. I haven't followed the rules of form, content or etiquette. And now, after all that failure, I don't seem to be much wiser. But I have finally created a novel that I think is salable, and I still don't know what the hell to do."

He smiled a slow, sad smile and nodded, "You got a big problem, but maybe I can help. I'll try to condense a lot of the stuff I picked up at USC. Here's the five-minute drill: First off, you don't rely on agents to sell your stuff."

"I don't?"

"No. You *find* an agent, but just put them on standby. Look, your first sale is probably going to be a paperback. You're gonna get $6,000 tops, out of which your agent's gonna get $600. How much overhead do you think a fancy New York agent can cover with $600?"

"Not a lot," I agreed. "But what do I do?"

"Simple. You go down to Crown Books. You're gonna aim for a paperback sale, 'cause it's ten times easier for an unpublished writer. At Crown, you pick out the five or ten paperbacks on the shelf that are closest to your novel. Write down the address of the publisher, make up some sort of a gushy-bullshit query letter and send it to the Submissions Editor."

"What do I say in the letter?"

"Tell the assholes how much you admire the work that they are doing, what an effect it's had on you. If it's on the top ten, say you can see why. If it isn't, say you can't see why it isn't. Praise the editor for his deep perception and the lasting worthiness of the stuff he's publishing."

"Isn't that a little...*thick?*"

"Naaa. They love that stuff."

"But I don't even know the editor's name."

"Easy. You get it by calling the publication house in New York. Then you send your manuscripts *with* your letter. Don't give the bastards a chance to say no without reading a few pages. Send them together."

I thanked Erich and headed over to Crown Books. Vietnam not being the hottest item (us having lost the war), I only found five publishers I thought might be interested. They were Zebra, Bantam, Doubleday, Ballantine, and Avon Books. I wrote my gushing query letter stating how affected I'd been by the work of these publishers, and how I'd written Crazyhead to fit perfectly with their existing line. Within a few months, four of them sent back my manuscript. Three sent form letters saying they didn't read unsolicited manuscripts. And the fourth sent a form letter saying the manuscript didn't fit with their present needs.

Six months went by, and I forgot about the fifth publisher. Until one day, out of the blue, the phone rang. I picked it up, and a rather detached voice on the other end of the world said, "Hello, Mr. Klawitter. This is Owen Lock, Senior Editor at Ballantine. We'd like to buy your book."

And they did, too.

On Writing Biblically

You may have noticed that a few of the sharp-eared political pundits of our age have begun to take Hillary Clinton to task for "speaking biblically", particularly when talking to audiences more or less solidly painted with people of color. Her grammar moves away from Karen Elizabeth Gordon's The Well-Tempered Sentence and Hillary's own more polished urbanity to sag into Deep South dialects. It's been called a lukewarm imitation of Martin Luther King, and that's one of the more polite observations. "We ain't gonna take it no more," Hillary warns. "We ain't gonna take it no more, no how," her voice moves up a notch, and then another, "We ain't gonna take it no way, no more, no how."

Now voices are easy if you're a writer; dialogue is always going on in your head. But my wife, who knows a lot of things, will be the first one to reprimand me if I go back to the old neighborhood in the South Chicago suburbs and start talking like an Italian-Polish-Jewish-German immigrant. "You're talking down to them," she'll say. "And they know it."

While she's right on this, the subject for writers goes a lot deeper than the spoken word. It is enormously difficult to convey dialect well in your writing.

229

Believe me, when trying to convey a deeply imbedded accent or manner of speaking, in general less is more, and it is very easy to fall off the turnip truck, as I believe the old ethnic saying goes.

I once fell badly off said truck with a writing project of mine, and it cost me four years of my writing life. It started in the early 90's. I was developing pilot shows for a friend of mine, and he invited me over to his place in Santa Monica. I showed up at his condo and, after a few minutes, his famous neighbor dropped by. Well, I didn't know he had a famous neighbor; but it was Deacon Jones, the National Football League many-times All-Star and Hall-of-Famer, a defensive end who had terrorized quarterbacks in the league throughout the 1960's and 70's.

We said polite things and then Deacon coughed a little in a throat-clearing way and said, "I read your novel."

That was a surprise. Crazyhead had come out in 1990, published by a small label in the giant Random House conglomerate and been pulled from the shelves as soon as the CIA got a look at it.

"Yeah, Ron here showed me." Deacon indicated my friend with a toss of one giant hand. I'm a normal-sized guy, and Deacon's hands were twice as big as mine. "I want to know," Deacon continued, "How come you don't do my life story?"

Well, one thing led to another, and I found myself over at the Deacon's place for a round of real Southern Black cooking. Deacon had been raised in poverty in rural Central Florida (back before Disney bought it all up and built a park there). When Deacon grew up, the black folks worked the fields, or if they could find a situation, they did what Deacon called "house niggering" for the white snowbirds who came south for the winter. Deacon's point was that the black man learned to survive on the white man's leftovers (a theme that would reverberate in the book we eventually wrote). The pork neck was dangerously bony, the pig's feet were about 85% pure fat and the pork and collard greens were bitter and greasy. Point well-taken. Apparently I was able to swallow the lesson to his satisfaction, because Deacon thundered, "You gonna be the man! You gonna immortalize the life story of the great Deacon Jones, the greatest defensive end the world has ever known!"

Well, I hit the books and the stacks in CSUN's library in the San Fernando Valley, and Deacon was indeed the greatest defensive end--and arguably the greatest defensive player--ever to pick up a football. I set up weekly meetings and began to listen to Deacon go through the salient points of his life and career. His rise from absolute poverty. His early anger at the white system. His college days--kicked out of two states for his civil rights activities, too poor to afford books (which he seldom, if ever, opened), finally ending his college football career being told to get on a bus and "never come back to Mississippi". His improbable drafting by the Rams. Early hazing by the whites, and the one shot that led to his rocket-like career. Wild times at the top. Big names, big games, stars, dope, the whole shot, but overall the context and turmoil of the times--Vietnam, civil unrest at home, Watts riots, Fearsome Foursome, big-time star...you get the picture.

Deacon is a great storyteller. He was born and raised in Eatonville, Florida, which as any black historian can tell you, is one of those rare towns with an unbroken heritage of black culture and tradition dating back to just after the Civil War when blacks incorporated the town as an all-black community. So he is in the tradition of Negroes who are great oral storytellers. He doesn't just talk biblically, he thinks biblically. Naturally, in writing his life story, I wrote it first person. I wrote it as an "as-told-to" biography, a common enough form of biography, particularly in the sports bio arena, and, believe me, that book thundered cover-to-cover.

But here's where I started to learn my costly lesson. When Deacon spoke, it was always with passion and with an overriding conviction in what he was saying. He has a great, deep voice and is wonderful to listen to, even when he's angry and yelling.

He and his wife Elizabeth came over one Christmas Eve, and the next day one of my sons said, "Dad, he yelled at you all evening!"

"No, son," I replied with a sad smile. "That's Deacon talking from the heart. He's angry, he feels life is unjust and that's the only way he knows." Actually, I thought that righteous anger might be good for the book. But I hadn't yet learned my lesson.

At the time, I was represented by Olga Wieser, a good New York literary agent, and she promptly sent the manuscript out to six publishers, then six more, and finally six more. All rejected the manuscript. Most said they wanted more sex, drugs and violence. But there was a second thread. Many of the editors complained about the tone of the book. Deacon, they said, came across as a braggart, an egotistical, selfish man, and even a liar. Nobody, they said, could have done the things he claimed he did.

After Olga gave up on the manuscript, I contacted Mike Hamilburg, a terrific L.A. agent who had strong ties to the big NY publishing houses. Mike proved to be a longtime fan of the Deacon, and our first meeting went beautifully, Mike gazing in wide-eyed wonder as Deacon dazzled him with stories from his storied past. (If any of you doubt the great man's oratorical powers, think back to the Hall of Fame invocation of a few years ago, when he gave the speech for George Allen's indoctrination into the Hall. That sound bite played around the country for weeks after.) The end result was that we formed a new team spearheaded by Hamilburg, and Mike promptly sent the manuscript to another dozen big-time publishers back East...with the same sad results.

There comes a time in every writer's life on every project when he has to face the harsh realities. Okay, maybe it wasn't the fact that Deacon refused to rat on his buddies and his famous ex-lovers with more explicit sex, drugs and violence. Maybe it was the writing.

Okay, but what about the writing? I did this for a living. I could stick subjects and predicates together with the best of them. What was I missing?

The answer came to me like a thunderbolt, came with such conviction that I spent the next four years of my life getting that project right. The voice, which sounded so right in my head, was coming out all wrong on the written page! I could do dialect and dialogue as well as anybody in Hollywood. I'd done script adaptations and animation and novels and short stories and documentaries and commercials...I'd worked with Leslie Nielsen and Natalie Wood and Rod Serling and Robert Lansing and Ray Bradbury and George Plimpton and dozens of other stars and personalities...but Deacon's dialect was so ingrained, his overtones and convictions so unique, that I can only describe it by saying he spoke--no, he actually *thought*--biblically all the time.

Now it's one thing to do a carefully building passage in a sermon that ends up thundering salvation or the fires of hell, but as a writer you can't do it all the time, paragraph after paragraph, chapter after chapter. At least I couldn't. Deacon was saying some serious and damaging things about bigotry in the National Football League and about the prejudices and weaknesses of the players themselves. And worse, those editors who were rejecting us were annoyed by the tone of what they were reading, as well as the content. In other words, I was writing about doubtful events in a manner that made them skeptical and angry. I was going to have to give up my "as-told-to" format and write a real biography. It could still be a "dramatic re-creation", but it couldn't be a first person narration.

This sounds easy; hell, just switch the voice and get on with it. But in practice, it turned out to be enormously time-consuming. Real biography doesn't rely simply on the recollections of the person whose life is being recorded...it has to be backed up by records, by facts, by data, and where possible by other people's opinions. And Deacon's recollections over time were swimmy at best. Sure, he did this or that incredible thing, but was it 1969 or 1970? Sure, there was a players' strike, but when, and exactly why did Deacon lead the charge?

I had to go back to the stacks and look at 14 years of sports pages spanning Deacon's career in the NFL. I had to interview hundreds of people--famous players of his era, sports writers, coaches, fans. I went to the Rams headquarters and read the play-by-plays, the recorded description of every play Deacon played in the NFL.

The book still had much of the flavor of Deacon. I even used first person passages at the end of every chapter, brief statements from Deacon saying what happened in his own words and others involved saying it was true or that he was an outright liar.

The finished work is titled HEADSLAP: The Life and Times of Deacon Jones, by John Klawitter and Deacon Jones. Since Olga and Mike were both burned out on the project, I sent it out myself, sent it to anybody I could find in the business, actually to over 70 publishers. We had several serious offers, and it was published by Prometheus Books in 1995, and the great sportswriter Jim Murray has called it one of the greatest sports bios ever written.

Deacon, of course, was tremendously pleased. We kicked off the book at the NFL Hall of Fame weekend in Akron in 1995. Deacon thundered, "We're gonna sell a million!"

Packaging Deacon

It was a year or two after the turning of the millennium. I remember this with some clarity because I'd done a Year 2000 calendar for Deacon Jones, the NFL Hall of Famer. I'd called it *The Streakin' Deacon Calendar* and it had sold well for his foundation, but by that time it was old news and Deacon was hinting around, wondering out loud how come nobody had done a major motion picture based on his mighty deeds both on and off the football field. Well, I'd written Headslap, the definitive biography of "his life and times", and I did believe there was some sort of movie in all that; and since I knew that Deacon knew I was pretty good at screenplay adaptations, I figured I'd better get working on it.

He always said he'd lived a really big life, and I'd always agreed with him. Turned out he was right; the way I worked it up, it was four major motion pictures. A saga to rival The Godfather or Rocky, only with footballs instead of murder and punching.

I sat down, outlined all four films and then wrote a first draft of the first one, and it worked out fairly decently. I mean, adaptation isn't as easy as it seems, but I had adapted screenplays before, and after all, I'd written the book on Deacon. The first of my epic quartet started with the Famous Headslapper confronting the ills of racial prejudice in Central Florida in the early 1950's. Born poor, raised poor, educated badly, he somehow gets one shot to try out for the Los Angeles Rams where he channels his anger and outrage of social injustice into football--and a legend is born.

Well, a decade before, when I researched and wrote Deacon's bio, nobody had wanted to buy it. I burned my way through two agents, Olga Wieser in New York and Mike Hamilburg here in Los Angeles. Publishers all said they wanted more sex, more drugs, more dirt on famous players and personalities. Deacon, who'd heartily engaged in more than his share of all those things, was looking to posterity and history. What's more, he was the head of the Deacon Jones Foundation, an organization established with Deacon's serious belief that the only way to fix inner city blight was to educate the children. Kids looked up to him. And that meant, among other things, that he wasn't going to drag his reputation through the muck for a few lousy bucks. I couldn't disagree with that. Hell, it was only money.

Long story short, after the agents gave up, I contacted over 150 publishers and finally managed to find Prometheus Books. They published Headslap in 1995. Famous sports writer Jim Murray proclaimed it one of the greatest sports bios ever written. Famous artist and documentary filmmaker Franklin McMahon said it filled in an important missing gap of American history, the racial blending of pro football set against the backdrop of the social unrest of the 1960's. Oh well, that and just over three dollars will buy any writer a latte at Starbucks.

Still, I'd done the screenplay adaptation and as it bounced around town, I thought we had a pretty good shot here and there. And of all the shots, I thought our best chance was at Disney Studios. Disney had come out with sports movies with uplifting endings practically since film had been invented. What was more, I'd worked on the lot at Burbank and knew people who had assumed positions of great power in *The House of the Duck & The Mouse*. In fact, I knew Dick Cook before he became head of Buena Vista, Disney's mighty distribution arm. Deacon felt the direct approach was the best one, so I prayed on old times and Dick got me a reading with the literary department, and wouldn't you know it, they *loved* the memory of the legendary old King of Sacks.

So it was with high hopes that I escorted my friend the great black giant to visit with the Disney story people. We went in through oversized doorways under a high arched roof held sturdy by columns shaped like the Seven Dwarves. The meeting started on a pleasant note. Disney was interested...but they wanted to see *the package*. Here I must confess that after all these years of writing, producing and directing, I should not have been--but was--at a loss. I hadn't thought of myself as a *packager*.

"What do you mean, *package?*" I blurted out. "We've got Deacon. We've got a great script. Nobody in this room disagrees, do they?"

Deacon certainly didn't. "Hey, man, it's me," he said, expanding biblically on his favorite subject. "I'm the best there ever was."

"Yes, no," the story guy said. "You *are* great. And it's a terrific project."

"Well then..." My voice trailed off. I guess I'm slow on the take. I should have attended all those classes on pitches and selling, instead of spending my time hunched over the keyboard. "But...*what*, then?"

"Well, you have to understand. We're the Walt Disney Studios. We've got ten great sports stories in the pipeline right now. Golf. Baseball. Hockey. Tennis. Even football."

Unbelievable as it sounds, I'd honestly forgotten about that. You know, you get wrapped up in your own great idea, and you forget there are hundreds of other talents out there, banging away at their keyboards, filling pages with stuff that is often quite as good as your own offering. Maybe even better.

"Oh..." I said. I think my mouth was hanging open.

Here it was, real life jumping out of the bushes to trip me up again. I think what happens is, as a writer, you concentrate on your own stuff, and when somebody says it's great, you somehow get the idea that's the whole story, you've got your ticket to the entire theme park, your passport to publication, your yellow brick road to success, your keys to the Emerald City.

The story guy must have seen my fumbling around, and he did try to help. After all, for all he knew I was Dick Cook's old friend, and held the deed to his mortgage or at least knew some embarrassing stories about the old days when the world was young.

"Look," he said, waving his hand at the mounds of scripts around him and the rows stacked on neat shelves on the walls. "We like your project, we really do. It's viable. But you've got to come up with something more, something to knock one of those other projects out of the lineup."

"Like what?" I wailed. "Deacon Jones isn't exactly chopped liver." I wouldn't have liked to have seen myself in the mirror at that moment. Grown men aren't supposed to blubber.

"Yeah, Deacon, sure, but..." The guy's voice drifted off as he thought about it. "I don't know...Denzel, maybe." He snapped his fingers and brightened at the prospect. This is what is known as packaging at the studio level. In a way, it's like fishing with somebody else's bait. Denzel Washington had just finished Remember The Titans for Disney and it had done good box office. On top of that, Denzel was Denzel, how could you go wrong?

I looked at the story guy. I didn't have anything polite to say. I was thinking, *And this is how these guys make the big bucks.* Sure; getting Denzel was a great idea. So was finding The Lost Dutchman Mine, but I didn't have a lost gold mine map. As it was, he could have picked up the phone himself, gotten right past Denzel's agents and every one of the forty-odd people who shield people like Mr. Washington from people he doesn't know.

"You're Disney, and you've just finished Titans, but you want me to take our project to Denzel."

"Right. Get Denzel interested and come back to us." He snapped his fingers again. "Or *Forty Acres.*" *Forty Acres and a Mule* was Spike Lee's company.

Deacon was looking at me like I was considerably further down the Hollywood food chain than he'd thought just a few minutes before. I guess it was the dazed expression on my face that gave it away, like a sea lion just after he's been hit by a killer whale. But Deacon was, as ever, fearless.

"I could get Denzel easy, but he can't play me," the big man said with a dismissive wave of one giant hand.

"Why can't he play you?" the story guy asked.

I'd gone over this before with Deacon.

"Too old," I cut in, before the great man had a chance to start in about Denzel having a big butt and us needing somebody with *quick moves* to play him.

"His company," the story guy said. "I meant his company. Denzel likes to direct. If he likes you, man, we can bump somebody, get you in the pipeline."

And with that, the meeting was over.

We squeezed our way out of the script-lined room and out the front entranceway while Dopey grinned and Sneezy sniffed down on us from high overhead.

We were on Mickey Lane, headed for guest parking. Deacon said, "I can get it to Denzel and Spike." But I knew he was speaking biblically again. He meant that I could use his name to call them, myself. I'd played that tarnished coin before, with mixed results.

Still, always the fool for the muse, over the next few months I did go back at it and I did use the Deacon's name as my calling card...with the same end result. By God, they love you when you're on the playing field, but the minute you retire you're ancient history. I pushed our project at Fox and Warner Brothers and a few indy companies, but the answer was always the same. *Attach name talent to your script and come back and see us, kid.*

Actually, I'm still trying. The script is out there today with an indy producer or two, and they've said they are *gonna let me know, kid.* That's the thing, you can never give up. I can't tell you how many pictures were doomed, damned and one step from the slush pile...and were rescued at the last minute, plucked from oblivion by some random twist of fate or otherwise innocent act of pure greed.

Some day you'll see <u>Headslap</u> up there in lights, and you'll remember this story. And when that day comes, maybe you'll also remember I told you that Hollywood doesn't have a system, it *is* a system. Maybe it looks like it is big, awkward, unreasonable and unworkable, but it's actually finely tuned to get rid of the quitters and the pests right away. If you want to succeed you've got to have staying power and they've got to like you. You can't go around yelling how great your ideas are. You've got to hang in there with grace and a certain sense of style. That means you've got to know you're good, and that so are a lot of other people. And most of all, you have to find a way to hop on the train. Find some excuse to barge in and impress an agent with a clown suit or a jackhammer or a ride on a balloon. Find a neighbor who's a reader over at Warner Brothers and bring him his mail (with your script slipped in the middle). Meet some producer by saying something nice about his kid at the spoiled little brat's birthday party, or ambush some hot actress with compliments at your local supermarket. "Oh, you like the *softer* brie, as well?" There is always a way, but it's usually not the one that seems to make the most sense. Find it, and when that doesn't work, try something else. After all, you're a storyteller. What else do you have to do until the Messiah comes?

Suspension of Disbelief

People like us...writers, that is, often discuss the reactive impulse we call "suspension of disbelief" as if we own it. We persist in this foolishness, and yet nothing could be further from the truth. The reality of the situation is that we are the original Doubting Thomases. We are dead last when it comes to suspending our own disbelief.

I suspect this is primarily because we consider ourselves expert storytellers. That fact alone should give you pause...we come to other people's stories on a busman's holiday. And when it comes to our own stories, that old devil ego is right there, standing between us and our own common sense. The true story expert is always your reader and your viewer, your common listener unqualified, compounded and multiplied to the n-th degree.

All this to say that what we do isn't easy and shouldn't be taken for granted. And to remind you to have a little graciousness and charity when you see holes in your fellow writer's script or story through which you might drive a truck. After all, the next writer coming up with a batch of laughingly obvious holes might well be, well, me...or, God forbid, even you.

I saw a movie the other day that left me pondering. It was called <u>Identity</u>, starring John Cusack, some other fine actors, and gallons of fake movie blood and other grizzly effects. The story structure--indeed, the premise of the movie--seemed so unsound that I wondered why some bold studio exec hadn't bothered to ask the writer what the hell it was all about.

Specifically, the movie's unresolved paradox is that murders are taking place in the killer's mind (though the viewer doesn't know it until the 8th reel, that is, near the end). You see, the killer suffers multiple personalities, and he doesn't know it. On one level of the story, call it the "real" level, he's brought to a last minute hearing to stay his execution...for murders which all take place at this desert motel while people are stranded in a violent rainstorm. Various possible killers emerge, but they all end up dead. Actually, only one lady lives, an ex-hooker taking her earnings and moving to Florida to buy an orange grove. Oh yeah, and a weird, suppressed fat kid.

Okay, let's assume that you're a very patient viewer; maybe you've got some problems with it, but you go along for the ride, to see what happens, if nothing else. (After all, it's pretty well-directed, a bumpy, messy horror flick complete with bodies thumped by cars and a bloody head in a laundry dryer.) But then, in the "real" story (the hearing), the killer finds out he has multiple personalities. The understanding psychiatrist explains that none of the murders were real, and convinces the killer that he has to kill his "killer" personality (from among his multiple personalities), so that he can find peace. None of those people he killed were real and the psychiatrist can prove it because they all had the same birthdate, were born in the same place, and so on. So the killer goes into his mind (back to the motel) and "kills" the guy we thought was the killer. The judge somehow understands he is "cured" and commutes the death sentence.

But then, the now-cured multiple personality guy is taken to a sanitarium, accompanied by a driver and his understanding psychiatrist. On the way, he kills the psychiatrist and the driver. Ha ha, fooled you, the killer was actually the little weird fat kid. And then the killer/little weird fat kid goes to Florida and kills the ex-hooker in her orange grove. Or maybe he just does that in his mind. Hell, by that time, who knows?

And by now another story problem has probably occurred to you--if the murders were imaginary, why was the murderer convicted? The judge says they are real--this guy is about to be put to death for killing six people at a motel. Ouch, which is it?

The writer will probably have an explanation for all this mucking about, and you can bet it will be complicated and include references to movies like Sixth Sense and Vanilla Sky...but you know the old saw--Pal, if you have to explain it, it ain't working.

My contention is that story is critical. Good storytelling may not be everything, but without it, you have nothing. And there's a fundamental relationship between sound story structure and success. You can prove it to yourself. Ignore what the critics say about any film or book. Go experience it yourself as a viewer or reader--instead of an expert. Suspend for the moment, if you can, your belief in your own supernatural abilities as a writer. This, as I often try to convince myself, isn't about you. Sit back, relax. Become an audience for a change. It doesn't matter if you're watching Steven Spielberg or reading John Grisham, if the holes in logic leave you gasping, if the plot doesn't hang together, if the action doesn't ring true, you can bet the storyteller's got a flop on his scorecard.

Bullfrog Speaks to Hemingway: A Few Words on the Importance of Genre

Everyone knows of Hemingway's famous passage with the man holding the ant-stick over the fire and how Gertie and the high snout members of the Paris Literary Clique made fun of the dull animal--Ernest, not the ants-- attempting to interpret the cosmic intention of a distant and uncaring deity. But hearsay has it the night he first thought about that passage was a memorable one for Mr. Hemingway. There he was, somewhere to the southwest of Paris in foggy Sarthe Province chasing the elusive trout, alone at night in the swampy woods, huddled about a campfire, holding an ant-covered stick and thinking about the Great War and those who had lived and those who had died.

Well, not quite alone. There was this damnable frog nearby calling, "Gud-i-grump, Gud-i-Grump, Gud-i-Grump!"

At first, Ernest thought it was some sort of mating call, but then, in his terrible state of mind, he came to believe the frog was saying, "Terr-i-ble, Terr-i-ble, Terr-i-ble!"

Finally, unable to stand it any longer, Ernest roared, "What is so goddamned terrible?!"

"Why, your writing ideas," the frog replied in a Bostonian accent. And with that, he hopped into the circle of light and onto the log next to where Ernest was sitting.

"Alright, where's your French accent?" Ernest said, immediately spotting the flaw. "And who are you, anyway?"

"This is a *magical* forest," the frog said, smoothly preening the place over each eye where his brows would have been if frogs had them, "And I have been sent here by Hold & Welch, publishers out of New York, Boston and London."

"What does H&W want with the likes of me?" Ernest grumbled. He was still feeling lousy from the latest gathering of the Left Bank Bunch. They had called his work "brutish mutterings". It had been behind his back, of course, but he'd been returning from the *pissoire* and had heard plenty enough.

"You may call me Tillie," the frog said. "And my masters at H&W wish you to write for them."

"Tillie? I thought you were a bullfrog."

"Sex is complicated," the frog said with a little sniff. "Now here's the thing, Hemsy, old boy: There's a whole new wave coming in publishing and we want you to get your woodie and ride on in there with the really big dudes."

"What is it...this new thing?" Hemingway said, looking around for another stick with some more ants on it.

"Our research has figured out there are only seven story ideas, and the writers who can pick one of the areas, master the formula and churn out the novels are going to rule the world!"

"Huh. Just seven...I don't believe it."

"Well, maybe about seven, more or less. Here: comic stories, love stories, serious stories, custom & manners stories, bodice rippers, crime stories and westerns!"

"Wouldn't a bodice ripper be a love story?"

"Don't quibble," the frog said. "Maybe it was something else. Adventure stories or something like that."

"A-hah! So there are more than seven!"

"The point is," the frog said, waving one green hand in the air as if he could dispel doubt and foretell the future, "we call these genre. From now on, everyone is going to write to specifications in each of the categories. It has not escaped our notice that you have been doing some fussing around in the war genre."

Ernest nodded, reviewing what the frog had said. It didn't seem to make sense to him. "Now there's a war genre," he said. "That would be eight. And, by the way, did you know H&W keeps sending me rejections?"

"Not anymore," the frog promised. "You're going to be very big in our stable, you'll be the H&W writerly dude in the war genre."

"I don't know..." Ernest found a stick with a beetle on it and held it toward the glowing bed of coals. He didn't think it worked as good as ants. Beetles had something about them that almost deserved the fire. "What do I have to do?"

"Nothing much different," the frog said, sitting up with a little businesslike sniff. "What kind of story you working on now?"

"Well, I've got this one about an American idealist who's running around Spain trying to fight Franco."

"Good, good." The frog gave him a wide-eyed, expectant look.

"He's helping the rebels and it's all very exciting. He falls in love and his girl gets pregnant. But then they are in a terrible mess and the only way to escape is to stay behind and hold off the advancing army troops. He's killed, but his sacrifice enables his girl and the freedom fighters to get away, to live to fight another day."

"Huh, not bad," the frog said, plucking some papers and a Waterman pen out of a slim valise he'd brought with him. "Sign here and we'll be on our way."

Ernest looked over the papers, "But this gives you the right to mess with my story."

"Not *mess* with it. Our editors will work with you to improve it to fit the genre. You see, we know what people want to read. We've researched it. Your story, for instance, is a sure hit. It's got everything people want--underdog appeal, romance, lusty bodice ripping, flying bullets, a brave and noble hero--it's a sure ticket, best-seller New York Times List, on its way, number one with a bullet. We'll have to change a few things, of course..."

"Like what?"

"Well, I don't think it's going to work with the hero fighting against Franco. Those were communists, right? Of course they were," he frowned and then continued without waiting for an answer. "And maybe the girl doesn't get pregnant. People don't want to read that. It brings up this whole abortion thing. They have sex, though. Plenty of thighs, good randy stuff. And...fix that ending."

"What about my ending?" Hemingway shouted in a hoarse voice. He was starting to look like he'd been run over by a road grader.

"Heavens to Mergatroid, no need to shout," the frog replied. "Just have the poor sap live. Look at the formula; you can't kill off your hero in the last scene. That makes all his sacrifice for nothing."

Poor Hemingway's dark and haunted gaze flickered here and there around the campsite. All he wanted was a stick, any stick, with or without ants. He clenched his fists and pounded his knees, but there wasn't a one in sight. He had burned all the sticks, and it seemed there was nothing left for it.

One loud but suddenly interrupted scream of protest penetrated the dense forest as Ernest grabbed Tillie by his smooth green waistcoat and threw him on the fiercely glowing coals. After that, the night was long and dark and quiet. Above the brooding man by the fire, and amazingly distant above the shroud of fog, the pitiless stars burned like quasi-eternal pricks of light. And, though it was a magical forest, this is a Hemingway story. So, if the Creator was watching, he didn't say anything.

On Giving It Away

If you're into podcasting, you know there's a running battle of words between people who put their writing up for free on the Internet and people who charge for it, no matter how little. While I think you can make a case either way, I really believe it's the writer's choice. If you're a great writer, sooner or later the public will find you...or they won't...and either way, in a hundred years or so you're dead, so what the hell are you worried about? Have another glass of wine, the full moon is coming up over Malibu Beach, you don't want to miss it.

I recently had a little experience with giving it away that may amuse you. Three years ago, I bought enough space on The Publishers Marketplace http://www.publishersmarketplace.com to publish my own tiny e-zine. I learned the basics of HTML and uploaded a masthead. (For those of you who may not know, that's the thing on the top of the front or "home" page that says who you are in a hopefully distinctive typeface: Newsweek. The New Yorker. Playboy. Amazon.com. Ask.com. Google.com.) My masthead was KLAWzine. My idea--not an entirely novel one--was to do a weekly e-zine that was interesting enough to be read, and yet promoted me in a professional way. In addition to my literary and film credits, each week I included a breezy blurb on what great new projects I was working on, a chapter of an unpublished book, and an unpublished short story, said last of which I literally have dozens and dozens.

Publishers Marketplace is an interesting and busy Internet junction where writers can connect with publishing professionals, so this didn't seem like an altogether backward idea. But after I'd been running The KLAWzine for maybe six months, a guy I know (Okay, it was a Hollywood agent) said to me, "So what's the big idea? Are you nuts or something, giving away chapters of The Heart of Desire? Look, budster, that's like giving away the cow." I think he meant, "like the cow giving away the milk for free," but I didn't say anything about that.

I knew this guy had irritable bowel syndrome, but still, I was surprised. I hadn't thought what I was doing was reason for anybody to get upset. On the other, err, intestine, Hollywood people do seem to go crazy over things you wouldn't ordinarily think counted for much of anything at all. I never thought twice about it. I usually adapt my unpublished novels (I have many) to screenplay format, and this guy had read my first draft screenplay, rejecting it as "not a star-power vehicle," which in ordinary language meant he didn't have any clients or know anybody who might be interested. In other words, a waste of his time.

"Christ," I said, "It was just chapters from my unpublished novel."

"Well, that's the dumbest thing I ever heard of."

"Hey, what do you care? You passed on the screenplay."

"Stick to the point," he growled. "Next thing you'll be giving free readings at the Starbucks across from ICM."

"Not a bad idea."

I tried to shrug it off, but mine wasn't really a very clever response, and he just shook his head and walked away.

That gave me pause. On the spot like that, I hadn't known what to say, but his little outburst set me to a bout of pondering. That's what my wife says I do best, mull and ponder, and she's right about a lot of things. There had to be some logical reason why I'd started The KLAWzine, but what was it? Why was I offering, week after week, chapters from The Heart of Desire, absolutely at no cost or obligation (as they say in direct marketing)? Instinct told me I was right, but I couldn't think of anything that didn't sound silly.

I was out walking Bucky, my hyper, shorthaired yellow lab, when the answer came to me. It was a gloomy morning in November, and as I reached a corner a few blocks from my house, I saw two young Hispanic gentlemen sitting on the curb. They had put off their sad chore of rubber-banding rolled-up hand pamphlets to doorknobs and were admiring a low rider parked in a driveway across the street from where they sat.

"Looks like rain," the one who spoke English said, flashing an $800 BriteSmile in my direction.

"Do you work in the rain?" I asked, a little wary of his oversized maroon windbreaker, too-tight orange Denver Broncos rip-stop sweatpants and too-friendly smile.

His companion, who looked like he wanted to start running before I might ask for his green card, started to shake his head no, but BriteSmile nodded enthusiastically. That made it one no and one yes.

"A human-man have got to eat," BrightSmile said. His gaze slid back to the low rider.

"That-there, yes, he do," I replied with a slow nod of my head. Maybe I forgot to mention, I'm also somewhat of a wise guy. People don't necessarily like me on the first pass. You have to get to know my inner beauty.

252

"This *excellente* car goes up and down." BrightSmile made a motion to indicate it had pump shocks. "It cost $3,000, I am sure..."

"How much do you make?" I asked.

His companion looked expectantly at him.

"Thirty dollar for six hour," he said, indicating himself and his partner. "These two of us."

I noticed he was wearing new running shoes with LED wink-lights on them. They actually sparkled red as he casually got to his feet, still looking at the car that went up and down.

Bucky was growling and looking like he thought they had no dog yummies and maybe switchblades meant for a human-man like me, so I bid the twosome goodbye and headed for Valley Circle Drive to check out whether the good lab and I might roust out a morning dove, a skunk or some other urban wild game. And somewhere in those moments as we walked away, the answer to the agent's question struck me in the back of the head like a Yellow Pages phone book.

Why was I offering any agent, editor or publisher who wanted to read them free episodes of my incredible thriller novel? Well, like BriteSmile and his nervous buddy, I was just out there casing the neighborhood.

Somewhere, Gutenberg Is Smiling

The East-Of-The-Hudson Literary Mob is quaking in terror. What is it, Mothra? A tsunami? A new Ice Age? A shortage of bagels and cream cheese? No, something even more frightening...It's you, ignoring them as you quietly go about your own business of writing and publishing what you want!

Have you noticed how a lot of people who make money off of writers are frightened out of their gourds by the new power in the hands of the scribblers of the world? That's the real reason why you're hearing all the nonsense about "legitimate" or "real" books, as if somehow everything else is a bastard publication. Look east, my friends. Hordes of old-fashioned agents, editors and publishers are trying their best to glare down their noses at writers who believe enough in their work to self-publish. You've seen it. You've felt their scorn. These guys all still bow to Connie, the great conglomerate god who has, until recently, ruled over publication of all literary works from exquisitely insightful poetry to books on how to fix your toilet.

There's nothing new, of course, about self-publication. It's the new technology that has these publishing industry fossils on the run. What makes it complicated for them is that there's not just one sea change, but two. First, with Print On Demand, a writer no longer has to mortgage the north forty to have his work published. And second, with the power of the Internet, writers no longer have to bow at the Manhattan altars to get their books to the people.

In truth, nobody's really been able to make the Internet churn out mass sales, but only a fool would deny that it's coming. Web ads. E-mail direct marketing. Links. Cross marketing between email and snailmail. Podcasts. Author's blog sites. It's getting better and better as we figure it out. Even best-selling authors like Michael Connelly and Nora Roberts are hedging their bets with their own easy-to-use websites, places where you can order one or all of their books without the hassle of driving over to the nearest Barnes & Noble.

The smarter editors and publishers, seeing what's coming, have adapted their services to what is a new gold mine. Some old, established publishing giants have even bought their own POD shops, hoping to jack the price or close them down. (You would too, if you were a brick-and-mortar Publishing House with your piece of the literary oligopoly to protect.) As for the rest, their criticisms are becoming more shrill as they are left behind in the horse-and-buggy days of publishing.

It's a wonderful age to be alive, isn't it?!

About the Author

John Klawitter has worked as a writer, producer and director. Based in Hollywood, he's worked for major studios, indy companies and run his own production company. He's written and produced for CBS, NBC, Disney, The Disney Channel, Paramount, Universal, Atlantis Productions, and many others. He has directed videos and films featuring a wide range of stars and personalities, including Bill Cosby, Ali MacGraw, Jane Alexander, Jacqueline Bisset, Ray Bradbury, George Plimpton, Leslie Nielsen, and many others.

Klawitter's first novel, an action/thriller titled CRAZYHEAD, came out in 1990 as an Ivy imprint published by Ballantine Books. He co-wrote HEADSLAP, the biography of the life and times of Deacon Jones (the NFL Hall of Famer and self-proclaimed King of Sacks), published in 1996 by Prometheus Books. Other published works include THE BOOK OF DEACON (Seven Locks Press, 2001) and TANS (a collection of recollections by the Old Spooks & Spies).

John Klawitter's books are available from bookstores and at www.amazon.com , http://www.bn.com, and www.double-dragon-ebooks.com More on him at www.johnklawitter.com.

JOHN KLAWITTER

www.ingramcontent.com/pod-product-compliance
Lightning Source LLC
Chambersburg PA
CBHW031543040426
42452CB00006B/166